D. L. Miller

Letters to the Young from the Old World

Notes of travel

D. L. Miller

Letters to the Young from the Old World
Notes of travel

ISBN/EAN: 9783337211875

Printed in Europe, USA, Canada, Australia, Japan

Cover: Foto ©Andreas Hilbeck / pixelio.de

More available books at **www.hansebooks.com**

LETTERS

TO

THE YOUNG

FROM THE

OLD WORLD:

NOTES OF TRAVEL

BY

Mrs. D. L. Miller.

Mount Morris, Ill.:
THE BRETHREN'S PUBLISHING COMPANY,
1894.

To

MY HUSBAND,

Whose Helpful Words have Encouraged me in my Work,

and to the

YOUNG PEOPLE AND CHILDREN,

Who Urged me Strongly

to Write,

THIS BOOK IS DEDICATED.

INTRODUCTION.

TWO years ago the author of this charming little volume happened in my office. I requested her to be seated, as I wanted to talk to her. I then told her that she had traveled much in this world, having visited Sweden, Denmark, Norway, Germany and the Bible Lands; that she had seen and heard much that would be interesting for others to read about, and I wanted her to write a series of articles for the *Young Disciple*, giving in the simplest way possible the information gathered during her travels.

"No, indeed," she quickly and positively replied. "I cannot do that." I told her I felt confident that she could prepare a number of articles, or letters, that would prove exceedingly interesting and profitable reading, and that the people were anxious to read what a woman had to say about the Bible Lands, the people and their customs. Repeating what she had said, she added that during all her travels she had not made one note, that she would have to depend entirely upon memory, and felt sure that she could not do justice to the undertaking. I urged her to give it a trial.

vi INTRODUCTION.

After a few weeks she handed me two letters. I examined them, and told her they were just what was desired, and that we would take as many more as she felt disposed to write. More than fifteen thousand readers of the *Young Disciple* know the result. For months they were delighted with these letters, and even before they were completed in the paper the author received many communications urging her to bring them out in book form. Many mothers wrote her and urged that the book should be published, that it was greatly needed, and would be the means of accomplishing much good among the children and young people. Even the children write sister Miller and insist upon her publishing her letters in a book. These requests became so urgent that the author finally decided to carefully revise the letters, write more fully on some points, and give the result of her labors in this neat little volume. We bespeak for it an extensive circulation, a careful reading and a wide field of usefulness.

J. H. MOORE.

Mt. Morris, Ill., Sept. 25, 1894.

TABLE OF CONTENTS.

CHAPTER I.

Across the Atlantic.—The Aller.—Small Sleeping Rooms.—A Singular Kitchen.—Last Farewell.—Seasickness.—Children on the Ship.—Four Little Boys.—Fog Horn.—The Lookout.—Icebergs. —A Little Sailor Boy.—Porpoises and Sea Gulls.—Taking on the Pilot.—Lights on the Other Shore.—Landing.............. 11

CHAPTER II.

Land.—Bremen.—On the Way to Denmark.—Copenhagen.—Religion of Denmark.—Singing.—A Farmhouse.—Malmo.—Market Place in Sweden.—Limhamn.—Fishermen and Boats.—Beautiful Lakes of Sweden.—Children in Sweden and their Bows.— Pine Branches.—Mother and Babe.—A Meal along the Way... 31

CHAPTER III.

Norway.—Kong Halfdan.—Fjords.—Hay Transfer.—Government Vessel.—Two Young Girls.—A Glacier.—The Captain's Kindness.—The Beautiful Picture.—Tromsö.—A Floating Buoy.— Eider Ducks.—Lapp Family.—Reindeer.—Torghatten.—Fish. —The Trap for Salmon.—Hammerfest.—The White Polar Bear. —The Drunken Sailor.—Arctic Ocean.—Whaling Station.—The Little White Church.—Striking a Reef of Rocks.............. 57

CHAPTER IV.

The Story of a German Boy.—The Priest.—Catholic Woman.—Corps of Singers.—My Singing Lesson.—Funeral Procession.—Children Playing.—Wooden Shoes.—Neatness of the German Children.—Their Politeness.—Cologne.—Its Cathedral.—Height of Towers.—Odd Costumes.—Art Gallery.—The Picture I Saw... 88

TABLE OF CONTENTS.

CHAPTER V.

Calais.—English Channel Experience.—Reaching the Pier.—Going Ashore.—London.—The Fog.—Show Lights.—British Museum. —National Gallery.—The Tricky Monkey.—Westminster Abbey.—The Tower 103

CHAPTER VI.

Venice.—A Gondola.—The Pigeons.—Trieste.—Piræus.—Athens.—Paul and Mars' Hill.—Sickness.—From Athens to Smyrna.—Man Overboard. — A Lesson of Unselfishness. — Smyrna. — A Cruel Father. — Ephesus. — Paul's Missionary Journey. — The Vesta.—Beyrut.—Jaffa Landing 117

CHAPTER VII.

Jaffa.—The Careless Camel.—Bible Characters who lived in Jaffa. —Jonah's Temptation. — On the Way to the Holy City. — An Arab and his Plow.—Ramleh.—Lydda in the Distance.—Leprous People Begging.—Leprous People of Bible Times.—Campfire in the Cave.—Jerusalem.—Our Room.—Solomon's Disobedience.—Tower of David.—The Stubborn Donkey.—Mohammedan Cemetery.—Mount of Olives 145

CHAPTER VIII.

Bethany. — Bethlehem. — Rachel's Tomb. — The Shepherd Boy.—Ruth and Naomi.— Garden of Gethsemane. — Departure from Jerusalem.—Yosef. — Jericho Road. — Ain-es-Sultan.—Morning Call.—Donkey Boy.—Dead Sea.—Along the Banks of the Jordan.—John the Baptist.—Bad Roads 168

CHAPTER IX.

Strange Kind of Fuel. — The Village Oven. — Women's Work.—Fresh Bread.—The Little Baby. — Landmarks.— Bethel.—My Faithful Friend.—A Trying Time in the Saddle.—Sinjal 196

CHAPTER X.

Shiloh.—Jacob's Well.—Tomb of Joseph.—Shechem. — Samaria.—Gibeah.—Dothan in the Distance.—Fountain of Gideon.—Shunem.—Shunammite's Son.—Nain 205

CHAPTER XI.

Riding into Nazareth.—Virgin's Fountain.—Tricky Horses.—Cana of Galilee.—Tiberias.—Story of Jesus and his Disciples.—Boat Ride on the Sea of Galilee.—Capernaum.—Mounting Horses.—Disappearance of the Dragoman.—A Serious Accident.—Lake Huleh.—Cesarea Philippi.—Mount Hermon.—Crossing the River Pharpar. — Damascus.—Via Recta. — Bible References to Courts.—Cup of Coffee.—Water Seller...................... 218

CHAPTER XII.

Farewell to Damascus.—Ain Fijeh.—Quarrelsome Arabs.—Onward to Baalbek.—A Friendly Arab Family.—On the Mountains of Lebanon.—Baalbek.—Rejected Stone.—From Baalbek to Beyrut.—My Horse John.—Homeward Bound..................... 243

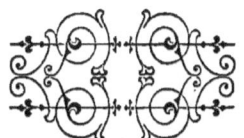

CHAPTER I.

Across the Atlantic.—The Aller.—Small Sleeping Rooms.—A Singular Kitchen.—Last Farewell.—Seasickness.— Children on the Ship.— Four Little Boys.—Fog Horn.—The Lookout.—Icebergs.—A Little Sailor Boy. — Porpoises and Sea Gulls. — Taking on the Pilot. — Lights on the Other Shore.—Landing.

AS a usual thing, boys and girls—and even older people—delight to hear about the ocean and the vessels which float upon it, and now I shall tell you what I know about the ocean and a voyage across it.

August is said to be one of the best summer months for ocean travel, because there are not so many hard storms during that month. There is very little use in paying attention to that saying, for the sea is just as liable to be rough and stormy one month as another. You know storms come up on land when we least expect them, and continue longer than we think they will? Well, just so it is on the ocean; so there is a possibility of having bad weather, go any month you will.

For a starting point you may choose one of four harbors,—Boston, Baltimore, Philadelphia or New York. The largest steamers, however, sail from New York, and it was from there that we took our departure the first day of August, 1891, at one o'clock P. M. The day was beautiful, just as clear as any August day you ever saw; so the hearts of the passengers were glad, for sunshine and mild weather were indications of a pleasant voyage, we thought. Pleasant weather on land, however, did not mean pleasant weather out at sea, as we found out later on.

The name of our steamer was the Aller. It is not one of the very largest ships, but it did seem immense to us. We were quite anxious to have a good look at our new home, so we went aboard long before sailing time, and before the rest of the passengers gathered together. In wandering around we saw narrow passageways and many very small rooms. In our houses at home we should have called them good sized closets, but in a steamship they were sleeping rooms, and plenty large enough—if only two persons occupied them. But it is a surprise to know that sometimes three and four persons must room together when there is a crowd. I am glad to say there was plenty of room on the Aller, and we were the only occupants of our stateroom.

In each of the rooms there was a sofa covered with plush, a wash-stand and basin, and two beds. The beds were built against one side of the little room, one above the other, and the person who occupied the upper berth found it necessary to climb up a stepladder every time he retired. Every piece of furniture was fastened securely; there seemed to be no danger of their moving from place to place when the sea grew wild and the vessel tumbled about. Each room had a window in it almost as large as a dinner plate, and just as round. The glass was set in a heavy brass frame, and a large screw was used to fasten the win-

The Aller.

dow. Not a drop of water could enter, no matter how high the waves rolled or how hard the water dashed against them. These windows are called portholes, and the little rooms are always known as staterooms. When a berth was spoken of we all knew it meant the bed. You see by this that the most familiar things had a different name on board a ship.

The floors of halls and staterooms were nicely carpeted, and we wondered how they could be kept looking so well. There was a beautifully furnished sitting room with carpet of velvet; heavy damask curtains, sofas of fine plush, and fine oil paintings decorated the sides and ceiling, painted there by a master hand. The comfort of the passengers seemed to have been studied well, for we saw there a beautiful piano and a library of books, all of which could be used by passengers when they felt so disposed.

The dining room and kitchen we found in the center of the ship, and the kitchen in particular interested us very much, for we had often wondered how the cooking utensils were kept in place when the sea became very rough. The mystery was easily solved, for on looking around we saw many racks which held the pots, pans and kettles firmly in place. Not very far from the kitchen was the pantry. There we saw plenty of glassware, and many dishes of different sizes, all nicely arranged in racks and fitting so tight that there seemed to be no chance for one of them to move from right to left.

But the time for sailing was nearer than we had any idea it was, and further investigation seemed out of the question; but before parting from our friends we decided that our floating home was neat and clean, and truly not an unpleasant place to spend the next ten days in.

Passengers were arriving fast by this time, and trunk after trunk was placed in the hold of the ship by diligent ship hands. We watched the people as they came aboard one by one. Some faces were looking happy, and others again showed marks of sadness. I wondered why there was such a difference, but concluded that the sad-faced people realized what a three thousand mile journey by water meant, and felt that they might nevermore behold the faces of loved ones again. If such should have been their thoughts, is it any wonder they looked sad?

All was hurry and confusion; the large bell rang, and "All ashore" was called out. Hurriedly friends bade each other good-bye, and those who were not to go with us made haste to leave the ship. The gang plank was removed, the ropes were untied, and slowly the ship Aller moved from the wharf. People who stood there waved handkerchiefs, and we watched them with our field glass until they seemed like mere specks in the distance. We were floating seaward, sure enough; and as the ship moved farther and farther from shore we continued standing on deck, wishing to see all we could of the land, for we knew many days would pass by when nothing but sky and water would be seen. In a very short time we were far from the noise and confusion, and not a strip of land was in sight; then, with tearful eyes, we left the deck and retired to our stateroom below. Our mind turned toward the sea and its dangers; visions of shipwrecks and collisions flitted back and forth before us; but trying hard to be brave, we cast such thoughts from our mind, consoling ourselves with the thought that millions of people had crossed the Atlantic safely, and perhaps we might be so blessed. Then, when we looked around and beheld the steamer with its immense engines and manned by such strong, hearty seamen, we could not help but feel that all would go well with us. So, after breathing a prayer for protection, we settled down to make the best of things, knowing the Lord to be our protector and feeling sure he would watch over and care for us.

The sea was not very rough and sailing was delightful. The ship rolled a little, but the passengers concluded the voyage would be a pleasant one. Ship acquaintances were soon made, our sitting places at table decided upon, and everything seemed to be in good running order, and we were as well fixed as it was possible to be while in the floating home.

After getting out to sea, one must get used to the rolling motion of the ship, and for many it means to get sick. Now, possibly, you have heard of people getting seasick. Well, I know all about it myself, and can tell you that it is a very disagreeable ailment. No one ever dies of seasickness, physicians say; so it is more distressing than dangerous. Many people, however, cross and recross the Atlantic without having unpleasant feelings in that direction; but, on the other hand, very many are unable to appear at meals regularly. You are not out at sea long until one by one passengers disappear. Some are missed but a day, while others do not put in an appearance during the journey. These last named never do get used to the uneasy, restless sea, and must therefore remain in their berths during the entire trip. Little boys and girls get very sick too, sometimes, but as a rule they are not as apt to get seasick as older people. While I know all about the malady, six days was the longest period of my affliction, and that occurred when in a hard storm a few years ago.

A sea voyage has a tendency to make one feel sad. You realize how great the force of water is and what a mere speck a human being is; each dash of the waves against the ship's sides brings you face to face with the fact that in a twinkling—if the Lord willed—the ship and all on board could be swept from the face of the water and their burial place be the bottom of the ocean. Some passengers bury their sad feelings in the wine cup and at the card table, while others go to the Lord in prayer. Which of these two ways do you consider to be the better one? The Lord does not like a drunkard, and you know drunkards cannot enter the kingdom of heaven. I hope you may all learn to love the Lord in youth, and may you never be known to drink strong beverages, or be found playing cards and gambling. Remember that all those who play cards and drink strong drink in youth usually continue it when they become men and women; for bad habits formed in youth are hard to overcome even in old age.

A great many children of all ages cross the Atlantic yearly with their parents, and some of them are very, very young, even tiny little babies with great long dresses.

These little ones, however, are never seen on deck, as a short time on deck would doubtless chill them completely and cause a spell of colic to follow shortly after.

The children who are old enough to run around have a delightful time playing on deck, and the nurse who cares for them has a hard time to keep them from getting hurt. The ship gives such heavy lurches that many times grown people find it a difficult matter to keep upon their feet.

Boys and girls as a rule enjoy a sea voyage immensely if they keep well, and not any of the passengers seemed more happy than they. When they were tumbled over by a lurch of the ship, it seemed like great fun, and jumping up they ran away laughing harder than ever.

There were four little boys belonging to two different families on board the Aller, and those little fellows attracted the attention of the passengers greatly. Two brothers were good, and two were naughty. The last named knew how to act ugly and be rude and boisterous; they quarreled with each other, and even spoke unkindly to their mamma, and, for that matter, to everybody else. It was plain that those boys had been spoiled at home, and that being the case nothing better need be expected of them when away from home. The people on board that steamer pronounced them both little nuisances, and wished they were at home; for how could they think of spending ten days in company with such children? But there was no help for it; so we all endured the trial. Their papa was one of the men who drank and gambled, and the mamma did not seem strong enough to manage such tough little fellows alone. The other two were quiet, innocent little boys, and when spoken to were sure to reply in a gentlemanly manner. Those who had charge of the two last named children were seen to pay a great deal of attention to t em; and will you be surprised when I tell you that even the passengers took pleasure in talking to those good little boys?

While writing this I wonder how many of you are like these little ones I am writing about. Well, I hope you are all like the good children, for I cannot bear to think of one of you as being rude and unkind. Do you want to be loved by those around you? Then be kind, loving, thoughtful children. You must not speak cross to mamma and papa; no, no; nor to grandpapa and grandma either. Don't say, "I won't," when asked to do a little favor, but rather run quickly, saying, "I will do anything you ask of me."

Did you ever think of how the Lord keeps a strict account of all we do and say? Well, he does, and it is written in a book, and then some day that book will be opened, and all the ugly things we have said and done will be read out. Just think how it will sound. Children, let us remember that the better we behave ourselves, the fewer will be the evil deeds recorded; and then let us remember, too, that the Lord loves dutiful children.

Have you ever heard of "fog at sea"? Well, sometimes it becomes very dense and you can scarcely see the full length of the ship. Seamen dread fog more than storms. It is then that the captain's face lengthens and his seat at table is vacant. There is great danger of collisions, for ships get nearer each other then, because they cannot see ahead. There is greater danger in going in and out of port when fog is dense, and many times have we read of steamers running into each other just as they were getting near to the stopping place. Such an occurrence usually means a great loss of life, for there is seldom time enough to save the unfortunate ones. The speed of a vessel should always be slackened when it is in a fog; but I am sorry to say that many of the captains are careless, as much so as engineers on our trains; they rush along anxious to make quick time, and if possible to gain port before ships of another line do. Many times they do gain port first, but it is the port of death; and we are made to think that the loss of life is a high price to pay for quick time.

We have been in fog a great many times. Once we were enveloped in it five days and five nights. All steamers sound the fog horn, and every few minutes during that time the disagreeable sound was heard. They gave it as a warning to other vessels, that they might keep away from them, thereby avoiding collisions.

There are always men on the lookout for danger. In a box way up in the rigging of the ship two men stand watching day and night, no difference how bad the weather is. Several men take their turn in watching, thus giving each one an opportunity to rest. If at any time there seems to be a suspicious object in their line of travel, the man calls out in loud tones, "Danger ahead." Sometimes the object seen proves to be a wreck, and if a signal of danger is seen, all haste is made to go to the rescue of those on board, and many lives are saved in that way. The box in which those men stand is called the "lookout box," and from it is called the hour of day. I remember so well of hearing them call the midnight hour time and again. It was called thus, "Twelve o'clock"; and then, "All is well." O what a satisfaction it always was to know that all was well; then after that call I was sure to fall into a sweet sleep, only to awaken at the dawn of another day.

Have you ever heard of an iceberg? Well, they are great mountains of floating ice which come down from Greenland, Spitzbergen, and other polar lands. Sometimes they appear right in a ship's course, and are not always seen by the naked eye. They float along for miles and miles under water, making it rather uncertain how close a ship is getting to them. Many icebergs, however, tower high above the water, and an account has been given of one seen a few years ago which was two and one-half miles long, two and one-fifth miles wide, and one hundred and fifty-three feet high. It is said that many million tons of ice were in that iceberg. When such an obstacle is seen there is cause for alarm, and well may the men on the lookout call, "Danger ahead!"

When the weather was favorable we sat on deck every day; and while sitting there we noticed a sailor go to the railing of the steamer with a canvas pail. We wondered what he intended doing, and so watched. He first fastened a long rope to the pail, then threw it overboard, and after it had floated about in the water a while he drew it toward him, lifting the pail over the railing brimful of water and immediately after thrusting a thermometer into it. We knew by that time that the sailor was testing the temperature of the water. He examined very closely how many degrees cold it was, then reported the result to the captain. When the water is many degrees colder than common it is quite possible that an iceberg is not far distant, so the ship's course is changed and possibly a wreck avoided. There seems to be no end of reasons why a man should be stationed to watch for danger day and night. If a lookout man could tell us the number of times he was the means of saving people from perishing by being the first to see the signal of distress, no doubt we should be surprised. Ships meet with accidents of different kinds. Sometimes we read of them burning up, and before help can reach them all on board are lost. How sad that seems. Think of the heartache of friends at home when the time for their return is at hand and they do not come.

The sailor's life is a hard one, and yet it is said he is not happy when off duty long at a time. Have you ever heard him called the "jolly sailor boy"? I have wondered why people speak of them as being jolly. To me they are a sad-faced set of men, and out at sea I never saw one of them smile; sometimes I wondered whether they knew how to. Perhaps all their smiling is engaged in when on land, where they get beer and strong drink.

Satan finds work for idle hands to do, and the captain is aware of that fact, so he manages to keep all hands busy when on a voyage, except during their hours of rest. You see if everybody is busy working or studying there is no time to plan naughty things, and Satan will soon find there is no chance for him. You would be surprised to know how many boys are learning to be sailors. Some of them on the Aller seemed not over twelve years of age. Their work is not of the hardest kind, still it is much harder than many of you are used to doing. It matters not how cold or rainy the weather, the little sailor boys, as well as the big sailors, must be on hand when duty demands them. It was no uncommon sight to see the little fellows out in stormy weather, and their hands almost stiff with cold. There was one boy who seemed to be on deck the greater part of the time. He was always armed with a broom, and he used it too; every little piece of paper, and every bit of dirt received his immediate attention, and with a steady sweep of the broom he sent them out to sea. These boys never talked with the passengers, but were polite when spoken to. No idling is allowed on shipboard, so the little fellows were busy and always on the move. Perhaps they would have enjoyed a good romp as well as any of you; but that was out of the question.

Sitting on deck is one of the pastimes of an ocean voyage. If a passenger seemed at all inclined to stay in the stateroom day after day when he was well and the weather was fine, you soon heard some one say, "Better stay on deck." The air of a stateroom is not fresh and bracing, and after having been on deck a few hours one has a dislike to stay in closer quarters. There are deck chairs to sit upon. Any person paying one dollar extra has the privilege of using one during the voyage. Sea air is usually a damp, cold air which makes it necessary to have heavy wraps and a good thick steamer rug to throw over the knees, that you may keep comfortable.

The first four or five days of an ocean voyage pass very slowly, for you remember there is nothing to be seen but sky and water. There was a strong desire on the part of the people to see a ship, and if some one should call out, "Oh, there's a sail!" all eyes were turned toward the dark object in the distance, and with the help of a field glass the outline of a vessel could be plainly seen. By and by it was in full view, and the children were heard to say, "Let me see too." You would be surprised to know for how long a time that ship is the subject of conversation. They wonder what her name is and to what port she is bound; whether she is a passenger steamer or carries freight alone. Passengers on a steamer are easily entertained, and no object is passed by unseen, for the most of them are on the watch.

By this time you can imagine us to be pretty well out at sea, and now the sight of a vessel is no uncommon occurrence. A sailing vessel, with her sails all filled with wind, was a beautiful sight, and scarcely a day passed without seeing one or more of them. Many, many years ago steamships were unknown, and a voyage across the Atlantic was not accomplished in as short a period of time as in these days. You know that when a vessel depends upon wind to move it along there is danger of its progress being hindered, for sometimes the wind is from the contrary direction.

Each day brought with it something new which amused the passengers. One day we found ourselves standing at the railing of the ship watching porpoises as they rushed along in the water below. Porpoises are of a sociable turn, and are seen swimming in schools close by the vessel's side. Their color is a dark gray, or almost black, and the under side of them approaches a pure white; their length when full grown is five feet or more. There was a time when the meat of porpoises was eaten and considered good; but now they are rarely if ever eaten; the blubber or fat alone is used for the oil which it contains. They are great fellows to spring up out of the water, and it is then that their full length and color are seen. That action greatly amused the children, and they called out, "O, look at the fish; just look at them!" And then the merry peals of laughter sounded throughout the ship. We never knew how long a time the porpoises traveled with us, for standing became tiresome, and one by one we turned away, leaving them without an admirer.

Sea gulls began flying about the ship by this time, and the indications were that land was not very far distant. How pleased we were to see them, and when land was mentioned our hearts swelled with joy. The gull is a webfooted sea fowl with long, narrow wings and straight beak, hooked at the tip. Occasionally you see some that are gray in color, but the most of them are all white. They feed upon fish, yet very willingly do they eat the scraps which the cooks throw to them.

Did you ever go fishing? Well, I'm very sure you had more trouble to catch fish than those gulls had. They would not be bothered with hook and line, and neither would you if it were possible for you to catch fish as they do. While flying above the water a sharp lookout is kept for fish below, and when one is seen they dart down upon it; and the next instant it is theirs. You would be surprised to see with what ease and grace they ride upon the waves, seemingly resting as comfortably as we who were upon the ship sitting in steamer chairs. We imagined they were tired, and that sitting on a wave was their method of resting, and a sort of pastime for them.

One of the great events of a sea voyage is the taking on of a pilot, and that occurs when a few days out from land. The pilot who brings a vessel across the Atlantic does not take it into the harbor, unless, as is sometimes the case, a pilot cannot be picked up because of the density of the fog. In that event the one who steers the ship across the ocean *must* take it into port; but he would rather not do so, for navigation is both difficult and dangerous the nearer one gets to land. The new pilot is taken aboard to superintend the steering of the vessel into port, and during the time he has charge of it the whole responsibility of getting her into port safely rests upon him. He knows where to locate the bad places, and makes a business of trying to escape them. Passengers watch faithfully for the appearance of the pilot boat, and a great deal of time is consumed in that way.

The pilot boat is small, and has one white sail; on the sail is painted a number in black. For instance, number nine, or number thirteen is to be seen plainly. The passengers sometimes thought the pilot boat was slow in putting in an appearance. They were over-anxious, you see; but in due time the little boat was seen away off in the distance bobbing up and down with the waves; sometimes it was lost sight of entirely; only for a little time, however, for the next wave brought it in full view, and a chorus of voices called out, "There she is, almost here." How small it seemed compared with the Aller, and the waves tossed it about as though it were a mere feather. At times they almost overwhelmed it; but the sturdy seamen had strong nerve, and they handled the little craft as though the task was a light one, still steering in the direction of the great Atlantic steamer. Can you imagine the boat coming nearer and nearer the Aller? I can; and in my mind I see the seamen throw the rope overboard to them; they catch it, are drawn closer and closer to the side of the great ship where the long rope ladder hangs. O how anxious we feel! What if he should make a misstep? And we turned away from the railing where the crowd stood watching. It took the man but a little while to climb to the top of the ladder, and before we were aware of it he was standing on deck. We looked at him with surprise, and he bade us the time of day.

No sooner was the new pilot on deck than we found ourselves steaming away. Just how soon he commenced work we do not know; but we settled down quietly, feeling satisfied that if all was well with us only a few days would pass before our feet would tread upon dry land again.

The sad faces took on a more cheerful look now, and peal after peal of laughter was heard. The piano was opened and lively music played; singing was engaged in, and indeed it seemed as though a new set of people had come forth. It was plainly to be seen that no one dreaded to reach land. The sea was rough, and the sky overcast with heavy clouds; but that was nothing new, for the whole ten days it was rainy, and the sun shone but little to cheer us on our way.

There was a band of music on board the steamer which played several times each day. Sometimes they played on deck, and always while we were eating dinner. Not everybody enjoyed their music, but since it was the custom to have band music they had to submit.

Sunday mornings we were always awakened by music which seemed in the distance; and the old familiar hymn of "Nearer, My God, to Thee," came to us seemingly from the far away. The sound of it never failed to bring tears to my eyes, for home loomed up before me, and I beheld loved ones gathered together for worship, singing songs of praise and thanksgiving. But the music passed away, and Sunday was spent just like all other days. Southampton, England, was reached, and there we unloaded some of our cargo. A great many passengers left and a few came aboard to go on to Bremen with us. Their journey seemed like a short one compared to the voyage which was just ending for the most of the passengers.

Between ten and eleven o'clock one night land was sighted, and many lights could be plainly seen along the shore, although it was said they were twenty-five or thirty miles away. We stood on deck an hour or more watching those beacon lights, and the tears of joy flowed down our cheeks. While we looked at them the beautiful hymn of P. P. Bliss, "Let the Lower Lights be Burning," came to our mind, and quietly we sang it; and I thought of this passage of Scripture, "Let your light so shine before men, that they may see your good works, and glorify your Father which is in heaven." And that night I realized what it meant for Christians to have their lamps trimmed and burning. We could not remain on deck longer, for the air was damp and chilly, so we retired to our stateroom feeling sure that on the morrow, if the Lord willed, our feet would again press mother earth.

The next day was disagreeable indeed, but when the time to go ashore was announced no one murmured. America seemed far, far away now, and instead of traveling under the stars and stripes of our mother country henceforth flags of other nations were to fly above us. Willingly did we journey to those foreign lands, so we made the best of the situation, deciding to see and learn all we could. There was a satisfaction in knowing that the Lord in whom we trusted would go with us in whatsoever land we journeyed.

CHAPTER II.

Land.—Bremen.—On the Way to Denmark.—Copenhagen.—Religion of Denmark.—Singing.—A Farmhouse.—Malmo.—Market Place in Sweden.—Limhamn.—Fishermen and Boats.—Beautiful Lakes of Sweden.—Children in Sweden and their Bows.—Pine Branches.—Mother and Babe.—A Meal along the Way.

NOW you may imagine us upon land, and what a change! The same sky with small patches of blue was above us, but the sea was all gone. Trees and grass never before looked more beautiful, and no doubt we appreciated the sight more because we had seen nothing green for so many days.

New sights and new scenes met our gaze, and, strangest of all, a new language was spoken; for you must remember we were upon German soil.

After having the baggage examined, which is always necessary when going into a strange country, we passed from the custom house to the train which was in waiting for all steamer passengers; and just as we were about to enter the cars there was a downpour of rain. There was nothing pleasant in that, but we had long since learned that there was no use to murmur when the weather was bad; so we settled back in our seats and watched the water as it came pouring down.

Between eight and nine o'clock that night we reached the city of Bremen. The depot was well lighted, and every one was enabled to see plainly where to go. Hotels were not scarce, for they are to be seen on all sides, so it took but a little time for us to find comfortable quarters.

How strange everything seemed! There was no need of watchfulness now, lest a lurch of the ship would give us an unexpected seat upon the floor. No noise of machinery sounded in our ears, and there was no restless, uneasy sea. "Give me land," I said; and who is there who would not rather be on land than water?

The next morning found us somewhat rested, and after eating a warm breakfast we planned for the rest of our journey. Time was precious, therefore it was out of the question for us to tarry long in Bremen; so as soon as possible we took our departure for Denmark.

Copenhagen was the first point aimed for, and we traveled northward, leaving Germany far behind. At Kiel we made our first stop, and there took a steamer crossing over to Korsör, which place we reached about seven o'clock next morning. A train was waiting to take all passengers on to Copenhagen, and about noon we had reached our journey's end.

Denmark is not a very large country, therefore it takes but a short time to travel from Germany to the north end of it. There is a great deal of water around this little country, consequently the air is damp and chilly most of the time, and people who live there wear heavy woolen clothing all the year round. Even though it was the month of August, we were quite comfortable in warm clothing.

We happened there just in time to have full benefit of the storms of wind and rain which are frequent during the months of July and August, and the changeable weather was in no wise agreeable to us.

Copenhagen is the capital of Denmark, and is therefore a very large city. We spent several days with the brethren and sisters there, for you know that is one of our mission points. Copenhagen is situated on the Island of Seeland, and so is entirely surrounded by water. The streets are very clean and the houses quite nice looking. There are little lakes in different parts of the city, and often the large white swans are seen swimming gracefully upon them, and people throw pieces of bread far out into the water so that they may have a long distance to swim before getting the wet morsel.

There were plenty of chances for sightseeing, and palaces, churches, hospitals, schools and museums were open to visitors special days in the week. There was not time to visit all of the above-named places, but we were sure that one week would be a short time to spend in the careful examination of all relics which were on exhibition.

The established religion of Denmark is Lutheran, but the Baptists and our Brethren are among the number who have regularly organized churches there. Instead of worshiping in fine large churches as do the Lutherans, they meet and worship in halls, for mission bands cannot afford to spend money to keep up large church edifices. Religious privileges are many, and yet many of the inhabitants live in sin and wickedness, turning a deaf ear to the pleading voice of the ministers.

Children who live in that large city do not have nice yards in which to play; but there are many very nice parks where they congregate every day and have the best kind of a time together.

The people were very kind to us, and no matter what hour we called upon them they were sure to give us a cup of good hot coffee. I wondered whether the coffeepot was kept upon the stove all the time, for only a few minutes passed between the time we entered their home and the presentation of the cup of coffee. Sometimes chocolate was given, but it was necessary to refuse one or the other of the drinks, so we gave the preference to coffee.

The Danes take great pleasure in singing, and I remember well, when we sat up until the clock struck two in the morning, singing out of the Gospel Hymns, they singing in Danish, and we singing in English.

We had a strong desire to see something of country life, so journeyed through the greater part of Denmark, stopping in villages and visiting at farmhouses. It was our happy privilege to become acquainted with a great many people, and we found them as kind and hospitable as those living in the city. A few visitors in a family seemed not to discommode the housewife, for no extra pains were taken to prepare fine meals. Company fared the same as those of the family, and none seemed tired by their much serving.

Danish Country Woman.

There was quite a company gathered together at one farmhouse, and we were among the number. When mealtime came not all of the people could be seated around the table, for it was too small, so eight of the number took places and the rest waited to eat at the second table. There was no nice white tablecloth to be seen, and not a fine display of nice dishes either; no silverware decorated that table, and, indeed, the whole house seemed void of an unnecessary thing.

But I'm going to tell you about the meal, so will pass by a description of the house and its furniture. On the table were a plate of black bread, a small dish of butter, and two earthen dishes filled with milk. The dishes were placed at the ends of the table, so that four persons could have easy access to them when the dipping-in time came. There were knives and spoons, but not enough to go around. Now what was to be done? Well, they were used a while by some, then passed on to be used by those who had none. We were strangers in the company, therefore the favored ones, so had the happy privilege of having a spoon all to ourselves. Now they were not of silver, as you might suppose, but bone. They were short in the handle and large in the bowl. Just look at your mother's kitchen spoons and I think the size will correspond very well with the bone ones we used.

Instead of having bread and milk, which most of the boys and girls like, we took the milk first, dipping into the earthen dish and placing the milk in the mouth spoonful by spoonful; and then we ate the bread afterward. Now that was no style of our own, for we followed the example of those around us, and the custom seemed indeed a very strange one. When the slices of black bread were gone, and the dishes of milk emptied, all stopped eating and thanks were returned to the Father above who provides so liberally. After this all retired from the table. We were not made comfortable by sitting on sofas and easy chairs. Oh no; but instead of that we had the privilege of standing until those at the second table were through eating, and even then we had the pleasure of being seated upon narrow benches, or possibly on an uncomfortable chair.

Those people had a novel way of, cleaning the spoons used in eating. I noticed with astonishment that after each person had finished the milk, and needed the spoon no longer, he took the bowl of the spoon between the thumb and fingers of the left hand, wiping it clean; after which the spoon was put away, to be used sometime in the future. Now, little girls,—you who do not fancy washing dishes, and especially spoons,—you must not adopt this method of cleaning them. But probably you will think about it as I do,—that the custom is not a nice one, and hardly worth following.

Houses in the country are built low and rather long. One end of them is used as living apartments and the other end for horses, cows and chickens. The farmer need not go far when feeding-time comes; it is only necessary for him to walk through the kitchen, open a door and commence his work of feeding. The odor of the stable permeates the entire house, and there is no way of getting where it is not.

Now some people think living close to a barn is healthful; but I must confess it is disagreeable in the extreme to me, and I had a great desire to be far away from such a nuisance.

The language of the Danes is quite unlike that of the Germans, and we were not able to talk to the people whom we met, unless it were through an interpreter, and that made it necessary for us to have an English-speaking person with us almost all of the time. To be in a country where one does not understand the language is quite unhandy, and yet there are a great many people who travel all over Europe and speak but one language, the English. Again, you meet persons who speak seven or eight different languages fluently.

There is a great deal to interest one while traveling through a strange country; but it is not well for us to write too much about one place, so we shall leave Denmark and go to Sweden.

Since Copenhagen is built on an island, you will know it is wholly surrounded by water. If such be the case, it is utterly impossible for any one to leave there for Sweden without going aboard a steamer. The passage of water between the two countries is called a sound, and every one knows it by the name of "The Sound."

One bright, beautiful day, in company with some Brethren, we crossed over the sound to the seaport town of Malmo, Sweden. The steamer was very clean, and the water unusually smooth that morning; so the ride of an hour and a half was a very enjoyable one. Malmo is only sixteen miles distant from Copenhagen, and when the day is clear the cities may be seen plainly when on the water.

The languages of Sweden and Denmark seemed alike to us, yet the natives claim there is quite a difference. Be that as it may, the people of both countries talk together and understand each other without much trouble. Our time was limited, and hurriedly we took in the sights, spending a short time with those of like precious faith who lived in the city. The time spent with them was well spent, for we were received cordially by all.

The cities of Europe are all very much alike; the houses are built in flats, having many families living under one roof. The streets are clean enough for footmen to walk upon, and there is no danger of even soiling the shoes. The store windows were tastefully arranged, being quite attractive to the passerby, and causing us to think that much time could be consumed in looking at the beautiful display of finery.

The market place of a large city in the Old Country was always attractive to us, and if it was at all possible we aimed to take a stroll through it. We admired the tastefully arranged stands of vegetables, crisp and green. Fruit seemed to be plentiful that year, and apples, pears and plums all looked beautiful. Even the butter, eggs and cheese stands looked well, and you would be surprised to know how many different kinds of cheese were on sale. Not much time was spent in looking at meats, fish and fowls, for close by was a greater attraction, that of the stand filled with flowers. There we saw the pleasant faced

Fishermen's Wives.

little pansy, the beautiful carnation pinks, and the loveliest of all flowers—the rose. I think I never saw such beauties as were offered for sale in the Malmo market. My husband—who was very indulgent—kept me well supplied with them, and their fragrance was enjoyed by others as well as myself.

Six miles distant from Malmo is a small village called Limhamn, and at that place there is a small church with a few members. We were requested to visit the members by way of encouragement; and as soon as the train was ready we started for that point. The ride was of short duration, yet very pleasant. Almost the entire distance the railroad track ran close to the water; so we had the pleasure of looking out upon the great body of water with its ships and sailboats.

The village of Limhamn is the home of many fishermen. About three o'clock in the afternoon they start out to fish. All night long they work hard, and in the morning often return with a very small catch. One time we looked out over the water and saw twenty boats of fishermen with sails well filled with wind. As a rule, those boats keep very close together, one following in the wake of the other. Sometimes the wind almost topples them over, but on they go, spinning along at a rapid rate. When the waves are lashed into fury by a storm many a little sailboat is turned over, and the boatman goes down, never to be seen again.

In those northern countries fishing is quite a business, and whole families sometimes engage in it. The women have a hard time, for they do double duty, that of looking after their families and then going to market day after day. After the husband returns in the early morning with his fish, the wife and all the children who are old enough arise and hasten to prepare them for market. As soon as fifty or one hundred fish have been made ready they are placed in a wheelbarrow, and the wife, after having changed her soiled dress for a clean one, trudges off to market, walking a mile or more with the heavy load. Where there are large families it takes many, many fish to pay for food and clothing, and it is therefore quite necessary that all should work.

The life of a fisherman is hard indeed; constantly dangers surround him; yet he seems to enjoy life about as well as those who work on land. They are strong, hearty looking fellows, which you will notice by looking at the picture of the four weather-beaten faces before you. Do you see their heavy coats? And then just look at the odd looking hat. The rim, which extends over the back of the neck, is for protection against wind and storm. Perhaps if we were upon the water that rim would be turned around and used as a protection for our eyes instead of the neck. After all, each fisherman probably knows best what is for his individual good, and no doubt the wind and stormy weather have taught him many good lessons on the preservation of health.

The time spent at each stopping place was of short duration; so then we left the fishermen at Limhamn to toil on, and we traveled still farther north.

Much of the country which we passed through was very rough looking, and yet there were parts of it which reminded us of northern Illinois, where we live. The greater part of Sweden is covered with forests of pine and fir trees, and the railroad ran through miles and miles of it, giving the passengers a splendid chance to see a great deal of country. There seemed scarcely an end to those beautiful trees, and we really grew tired looking at them for hours at a time.

Sweden is noted for her many beautiful lakes. Some of them are quite large, and boats are seen upon them; but very many of them are small. We passed alternately forests and lakes, and we were always sure to see a forest after having passed a lake. Never before in my life had I seen as many beautiful lakes as we saw during that ride.

Sometimes for miles and miles the ground was covered with heather, or ling. Its leaves are very small, and they are green all the year round. It bears very pretty little flowers; some are white and some are pink. They are not at all fragrant, but very pretty to look at. Heather is of no use to the farmer, and no doubt he would rather not have it cumber his ground. But the train comes to a halt, and we leave it, expecting to visit in the country, and thereby come in closer contact with the people.

As a rule the Swedish people are religiously inclined, and they esteem it a great pleasure to have the story of Jesus and his love told them. Many times I noticed the tears chase each other down their weather-beaten faces while the minister talked about the saints of old. Very willing and

Fishermen.

anxious were they for the Word of God; and I'm so glad to tell you it was given them in all of its purity.

The women seemed sorrowful because I could not converse with them; and in turn I felt sorry not to be able to gratify their desire; but we got along nicely anyway. Their hearts seemed full of love for me, and they made it manifest by patting me upon the shoulder, squeezing my hand, and kissing me frequently. It was all they could do, and I did not object. You must remember these people lived on farms, were very poor, and knew nothing of the ways of the world as we know them. They were innocent, kind-hearted and good.

I have often wished, since writing these little letters, that I could have talked with the children in those far-away countries. There might have been many things to tell which would have pleased you. But we are deprived of much pleasure as we pass through this world; and, since it cannot be otherwise, we must be satisfied.

Children in Sweden are like other children; they talk, laugh, and romp too. We longed to talk with them, but that being out of the question we undertook to make them understand us by making gestures, and that method was quite interesting. Now, children, whenever you are in a position where you cannot talk to those around you, just try my plan, and see how nicely you will get along.

Children enjoy doing favors for those who are older than themselves; and how much they love to be praised for it! Now that brings to my mind the little Swedish girl who took great pleasure in gathering plums and bringing them to the house. After having sorted them, the largest and nicest ones were handed to me. In her language I thanked her, but that was all I was able to say. No doubt she wished I'd talk a little more to her; but, finding my list of words was very short, she concluded to do all the talking herself, so chattered away at a lively rate, not even waiting for an answer. I could do nothing but look and listen. We were very good friends anyway, and each talked to the other in her own native language, but neither understood a word that was spoken by the other. How would you like to live with people and not be able to talk with them? The home of my little friend was our home for at least two weeks, and before we bade them adieu I had wandered with her from orchard to barn, and from one neighbor's house to another; and when the heavy wind had shaken down the beautiful apples, together we picked them up. Going from place to place with the little girl helped me pass away many lonely hours, and I assure you that not many hours passed without my longing for the friends at home. Do you wonder then that so small a thing would give me pleasure?

In Sweden the little girls—and women too—make such pretty little bows. Not as we bow in America; no, but with a very quick and graceful movement. There is a bending of the knee, and a dropping of the body. Old women, young women, and even tiny little girls, all bow exactly alike. It took quite an effort on my part to keep back the smile which wanted so much to come, and I'm sure you would have had the same feeling if you could have seen them. From infancy children are trained to have respect for older people, and it is taught them in such a way that they never forget it. They were taught to bow; that was a mark of courtesy and respect. Will you, my little readers, try to remember the training given at home, as do the children away across the ocean?

I told you there were miles and miles of pine forests in Sweden, you remember? Well, physicians recommend persons who have weak lungs to take many, many rides through them, claiming that the pine odor is healing to the lungs. I do not know how much truth there is in the saying, for our lungs seemed all right; but I do know that a ride through the forests in a wagon is delightful, and worth taking.

Pine branches are used quite profusely in that country for decorating both the inside and outside of houses on special occasions. One time we were expected at a certain country home, and great preparations had been made for our reception. The hostess did not bake fine cakes or kill chickens for us, either. Well, what did they do? Why, they took a jaunt to the forest, gathered evergreens—pine branches—ever so much of them, took them home, cut them up in many small pieces, and scattered them on the walk from the gate where we were to dismount up to the house, then almost covered the steps leading to the front door. Two beautiful young pine trees had been planted, temporarily, on either side of the steps, and indeed the old farmhouse took on quite a pleasant appearance. In walking over the fresh-cut pine its odor came up around us, and was quite agreeable. Now don't you think those people were kind? Perhaps when I tell you that all of the work was done by women and children you will think we would be strange people not to feel pleased with such a reception. We enjoyed all, for we felt sure that love for the American wanderers prompted them to work so hard.

Soon we shall leave this interesting country; but before we do so will call your attention to the picture of a Swedish mother and babe. Do you notice the pleasant looking faces of both parties? Then observe closely the peculiar way of dressing. That woman doesn't need a baby carriage to haul the little one in; no, indeed; she has something better, for with the child sitting in the sling which hangs over the shoulder the mother's hands are free and she uses them to knit stockings for the rest of the family. That way of dressing is not altogether in vogue now, for fashion has gone ahead and the modest apparel like that of the woman in the picture is very seldom seen these days.

We are admonished to love those who are of the same household of faith, and as the family with whom we stayed belonged to the same communion as ourselves, we had much love in our hearts for them. With tearful eyes the farewells were said, and we wondered whether the Lord in his goodness would permit all to meet again this side of the grave.

Time passes swiftly, no matter where you are, at home or in a foreign land, so the allotted time for rest in Sweden had finally come to an end. There were many days of

Swedish Mother and Child.

travel before us, and riding becomes quite tiresome when day after day is spent in foreign railway carriages.

Our new-made friends were loath to have us leave, and farewell seemed a hard word for them to say. Several accompanied us to the station, many of them walking in the hot sun a distance of two or three miles. We took seats at the window of the car, and when the train passed out we looked back and saw them waving handkerchiefs until the distance widened between us and the flutter of white was no more visible. Waving the handkerchief after departing friends is a custom of the country, and at every station along the railroad it is seen.

There are a number of things along the line of travel to interest tourists, if they are in the proper mood to be interested. Many days of continued travel bring with them feelings of weariness; and when that is the case, beautiful scenery or odd customs of the people fail to attract attention. The discomforts of foreign travel are many, and they often drive away the enthusiastic feelings one had in the beginning of a long journey.

The guard of a train usually takes orders for meals which passengers expect to get along the road, and when you are not thinking of it he puts his head in at the window and asks who among the number desire dinner. A dispatch is sent, and the meal is ready by the time we reach the stopping place.

You enter a nice, clean dining room, and there you see tables spread with very white tablecloths. Here and there upon the tables are stacks of soup plates, dinner plates and small dessert plates, and knives, forks and spoons close by them; dishes of boiled salmon with sauce, hot potatoes, boiled beef and cauliflower with cream sauce; then, too, ever so many kinds of cheese, and some smoked meats.

We followed the example of the rest of the people, and forthwith helped ourselves to a plate, knife, fork and spoon. No waiters looked after our wants, so each person looked after himself, being careful not to push or elbow his neighbor. Everybody was orderly, and the dinner was splendid. Two women had the oversight of the dining room, but they sat off at one side, behind a little table, and did not leave their seats until paying time came, when they took the money and made the change.

A servant appeared and took away each plate when it was needed no more, and when time for the dessert had come, she removed the fish, meat and vegetable dishes. There was no tarrying one for the other, but as each person desired a dessert he arose, took a plate and helped himself to the jellied raspberry juice, or tapioca pudding; and as a dressing for them delicious whipped cream, poured from a large glass pitcher, was used. After paying the bill, each one passed out to the train, which started soon after.

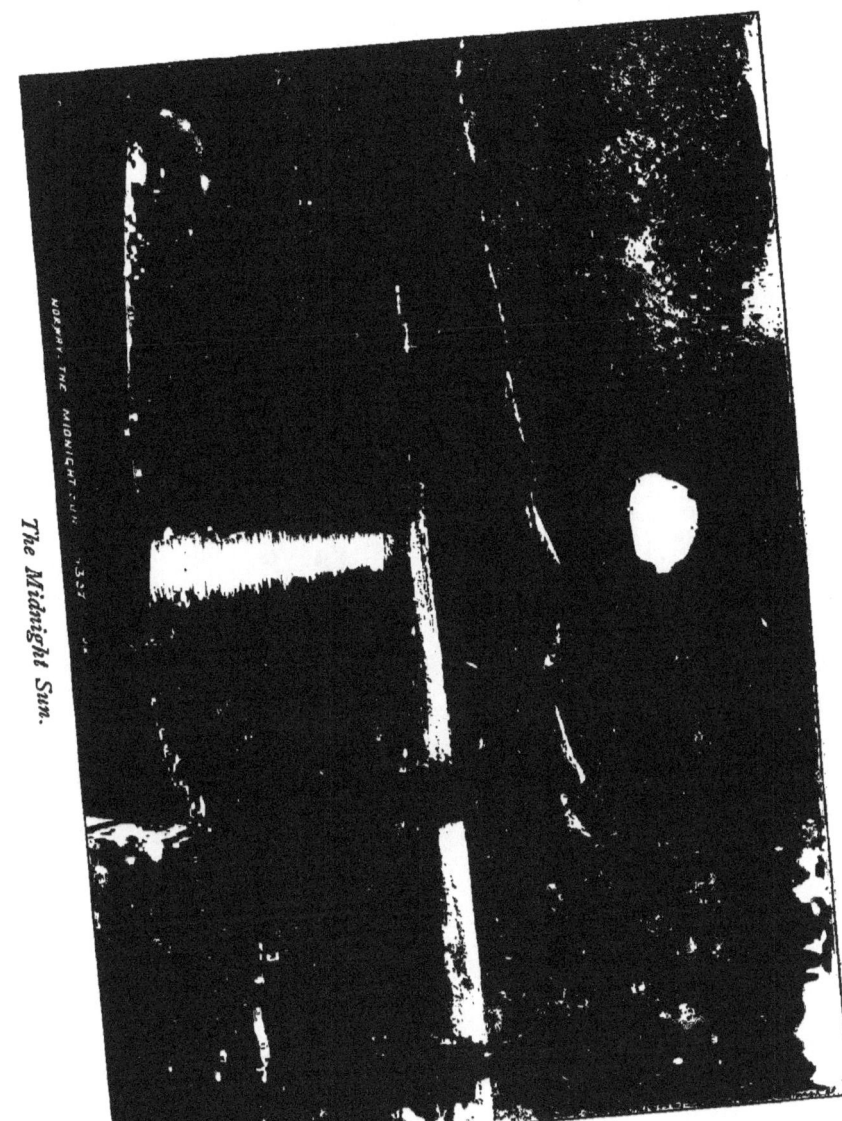

The Midnight Sun.

CHAPTER III.

Norway.—Kong Halfdan.—Fjords.—Hay Transfer.—Government Vessel.—Two Young Girls.—A Glacier.—The Captain's Kindness.—The Beautiful Picture.—Tromsö.—A Floating Buoy.—Eider Ducks.—Lapp Family.—Reindeer.—Torghatten.—Fish.—The Trap for Salmon.—Hammerfest.—The White Polar Bear.—The Drunken Sailor.—Arctic Ocean.—Whaling Station.—The Little White Church.—Striking a Reef of Rocks.

BEFORE a tourist leaves home the mind is usually settled upon certain places to be visited in the Old World. We think it a very good plan, for then the history of those special points may be looked up and the visit made more satisfactory; for the more knowledge one has of noted historical places, the more pleasing is the visit.

Norway was the country we had decided to visit, and "The Land of the Midnight Sun" was the point aimed for. So the twentieth day of August found us two in the city of Throndhjem, once the capital of Norway. Instead of railway coaches, passage was taken on a steamer which was then at the pier puffing heavy black smoke from the smokestack.

The sailors were busily engaged in storing away the cargo, and there was every indication that in a few hours she would steam out of port. Upon inquiry we found that steamers had quit running to that far northern point; the season being over, there would be no more chance for us that year. That information was quite disappointing, for we had looked forward with a great deal of pleasure to the time when we should look upon the bright sun shining at midnight. The fault seemed to be our own, for we had not started north soon enough. We concluded to go as far as the steamer went, rather than turn back; so the tickets were purchased and a stateroom procured on board the steamer Kong Halfdan.

The name seemed odd indeed, and you cannot imagine how very small the ship did seem compared to the monsters on the Atlantic. I did wish it were larger, though; but since it was not in my power to change its size I just tried to appear unconcerned, and that wasn't a very easy task. This vessel belonged to the government, and in the season she made regular trips between Throndhjem and North Cape. As the steamer was not to leave her pier for an hour or more, we decided to walk around the city and thus escape the noise and confusion of loading, which was in full operation all around. Walking seemed to be a tiresome piece of work that morning, and we were glad to return and take a seat upon deck, where we remained until sailing time.

The day was cloudy, with a stiff sea breeze blowing and we concluded a good shaking up was in store for us; perhaps a spell of seasickness in the bargain. The captain said, "Nobody ever gets seasick on the fjords of Norway"; but I decided to wait and see. The water in the bay was rough, and the ship inclined to roll a little, so the outlook did not seem very flattering.

The time for sailing came, and at twelve o'clock, noon, the anchor was drawn up, and quickly we left the pier. I sat on deck but a short time, for the rocking motion of the ship gave my stomach an unsettled feeling; so, as soon as possible, I withdrew to my stateroom, and in a short time thereafter my head was upon a pillow, where the sight of water was entirely shut off.

After having gone a few miles, we were agreeably surprised at finding a calm, beautiful sea. The clouds passed away, and the sun in all its splendor shone down upon us, and each day, from that time on, the sun cheered our way. We were out for a twelve days' cruise along the rocky coast of Norway, and you can imagine it was pleasing to have fine weather and a smooth sea.

There were not many first cabin passengers on board the Kong Halfdan, and it so happened that I was the only lady; but that which disturbed me the most was to know that among them all we were the only two who were English-speaking. The captain, who was a very nice man and extremely kind to us, talked English quite well, so every once in a while we held a conversation with him.

The captain and first and second mate ate at the same table with the passengers. It was a long, narrow table and accommodated sixteen people. A lounge ran the full length of one side of it, while chairs were used on the other side. Each one had his seat, and at every meal we sat in the same places. The captain was seated to the right and my husband to the left of me, and from there down others sat; but we had the honor of being seated on the lounge, and near to the captain.

The fjords of Norway are known as arms of the sea, they being a part of the Atlantic and Arctic oceans. Some of the fjords are narrow, but others are quite wide. Large vessels float upon them, for the water is very, very deep.

The Norwegians are a thrifty people, and their little homes on the green hillside along the fjords were very inviting as we passed them one by one. Some were near enough for us to see the chickens picking and scratching in the yard, and gladly would we have exchanged our stateroom on the steamer for a cozy room in a cottage.

The steamer had regular stopping places called stations along the line, and at those places they took on passengers and cargo. There was no chance to cast anchor close to shore, for rocks run far out into the water. Passengers and freight were always taken off in rowboats. Mountains seemed to hem us in, and the splendid scenery was a surprise to us; yet it proved to be quite a monotonous ride and we were anxious for a change.

Green fields were scarcely ever seen, but small patches of green were noticed here and there on the sides of the mountains. I wondered what the Norwegians would say if a glance at fields of grass and grain, as we know them, could be placed before them.

A familiar object along the way was a wire stretched from the foot to the summit of a mountain. I'll call it a hay telegraph. You see the farmer cuts grass which grows on narrow ledges of rocks way up in the mountain. He stores it away until great quantities have been accumulated and then, when ready to have it stored close to his house for winter use, he sends bundle after bundle down the wire. That wire was a novel contrivance to save labor, for without it very many steps would surely have to be taken by the weary farmer.

The government vessels carry provision and mail to the inhabitants living along the coast, and we were reminded of our freight or express cars, carrying all kinds of things and delivering them at regular points along the line. The steamer did not present a beautiful appearance, for the deck was greasy and very dirty looking. Quite a smell of fish filled the air, and we found that her main cargo consisted of fish and fish-oil. All of this accounted for the greasy look of the deck and the bad odor which greeted our nostrils. You would be surprised to know how much freight and express is taken on and off at those stations. I passed many hours standing at the railing of the ship watching the process of loading and unloading baggage, passengers and freight, and felt myself well entertained.

One time two young girls rowed up alongside of the Kong Halfdan. A rope from the ship was thrown them with which to steady themselves; they caught it and were just in the act of taking hold of their express package when a wave came and washed them back; the second attempt was made, and that time they caught the rope and held tight to it. Do you believe they were scared? Well, they were not; and instead of screaming and saying, "We shall drown. Oh, don't let us try it again!" they pulled at the oars, and with a merry laugh received the package and then rowed for the shore, laughing and talking. Their package was a guitar, and no doubt the pleasure of having the instrument caused them to row with energy. Women and girls can handle a boat about as well as a man, and they have no more fears of being on water than the farmer's daughter has when riding upon the back of a horse.

At almost every station passengers came aboard, and oh how much we did wish English-speaking people would be of the number, for we did so long to hear our native language spoken. Almost all who took passage on our ship went second cabin. The fare was cheaper and the accommodations accordingly poorer than first cabin. Foreigners don't mind poor accommodations; they are used to them at home, and it would be useless to pay a high price for anything better than what they are used to.

As we traveled on the scenery seemed more grand; mountain peak after mountain peak was seen in the distance, and the captain, who was always ready to give us information, said, "Snow is seen upon those mountains the entire year, and numerous glaciers are sent off on both sides, extending very nearly down to the sea." Now a glacier is an immense mass of snow and ice formed in the regions of perpetual snow. It moves down, down the mountain side, carrying large rocks along. Would you like to see one? From the steamer we saw the snow-capped mountains, but a glacier we never beheld. The cold air which comes from a field of snow and ice blew down upon us as we stood upon deck, and I drew my heavy winter shawl more closely about me. The highest of the mountains which I've been telling you about are said to be five thousand feet high. Is it any wonder that we saw them when far away?

I told you the captain was kind and thoughtful. Well, one day he gave us a surprise by running his vessel out of its course into a very narrow fjord. When he knew we were desirous of seeing things of interest along the route, he aimed to gratify the wish if possible. Our captain was proud of the scenery of Norway, and whenever he could make time and get to the different stations when due he showed his passengers favors.

All first cabin passengers were invited to go up on the bridge. Now, that is where the steersman stands to guide the vessel. There was not a thing to obstruct the view either ahead or to the right or left of us; and everybody seemed to be amazed at the outlook. By and by the ship was steered toward a very narrow looking place, and I said, "Why, you won't try to go through there, will you?" and before my question was answered the ship passed between two high mountains into a small body of water which seemed scarcely large enough to hold a vessel the size of the Kong Halfdan. Oh what a picture! It was beautiful! There was the blue sky overhead, with mountains on both sides of us, and not far away a lovely waterfall. There was a splendid echo at that point, and when the captain told us that the mountain to the right was twelve hundred feet high there was a return sound which repeated the words. The waterfall was fed from the melting snow of the mountains, and it was a pleasure to watch the water rush and tumble down the mountain side. The little stones which lay in its way seemed not to hinder the rushing water, and if perchance they became loosened all went tumbling together until the water below was reached, when the stones fell to the bottom, never to rise again.

While the beautiful picture was being admired the captain blew the steam whistle three or four times, and as the shrill sound was quite unexpected to us some screamed out loud, and everybody within hearing distance laughed.

We had not time to tarry long at that place, for it was getting on toward sundown. It seemed to me the ship was handled as though she were a mere toy, and the first thing we knew she had been turned around and was out in the wide fjord, steaming along at a rapid rate. One by one we took the captain by the hand and thanked him for the pleasure he had given us. You see, boys and girls, everybody likes to be appreciated, even the captain of a steamship; and when we saw the weather-beaten face all smiles we felt pretty sure we had given the captain some pleasure too, for he knew that the extra pains he had taken was gratifying to every one of the passengers.

Tromsö is the name of one of the stations along the route, and there we cast anchor lying by eight hours. All of the passengers but myself went ashore, and the captain said, "What, don't you go too? It will be lonely without the rest of the people." But I concluded it would be more pleasant to remain on the steamer and write letters than to go ashore in a small boat, for somehow I never did fancy the getting in and out of a small rowboat. My letter writing occupied several hours, and when I had finished I went on deck where there was enough to entertain me the rest of the time. Coal, freight and passengers were taken on at Tromsö, and for a while all was noise and confusion.

Not very far from the ship was a floating buoy. Now, that is a floating mark to point out the position of objects beneath the water, such as rocks, sandbars, and anything which might prove disastrous to vessels or small boats. There are many different kinds of buoys, and each one has a meaning. The seaman knows them all and reads them like a book.

Out in the bay were a great many little rowboats. One of them attracted my attention because there were three little boys in it, and I thought, "How dangerous!" I watched them, however, and saw they were making for the buoy. By and by they were alongside of it, and the next thing I knew two of them were sitting astride of it, while the third kept the boat from drifting away. Now I had decided those little fellows would surely roll off and perhaps be drowned, and I grew very anxious about their safety; but after having watched them an hour I concluded they were not strangers on the water, but knew the buoy well and were used to playing just where it pleased them.

Their stay was a long one, and not wishing to watch them longer I turned to the other side of the deck; and there in the water were a dozen or more eider ducks swimming along as gracefully as could be, seeming not one bit afraid of the people who rowed past them. Eider ducks frequent low, rocky places near the coast. Their down is in great demand; it is used in that country for filling bed-coverlets, and you would be surprised to know how light in weight coverlets filled with eider down are. During the breeding season no one is allowed to shoot the eider ducks, or even to fire off a gun near their nests. Persons who are thoughtless enough to do so are fined for it. Because of the great care taken they are very tame, and do not fear man when he comes near them.

The sun was getting pretty low, and the time for starting was near at hand. I was still on deck, but now my eyes were cast in the direction of the city. I was looking for a boat that would bring back the passengers who had gone ashore. In the distance a boat came in view, and taking the field glass which was near by I pointed it in that direction; and there, sure enough, was the one I had been looking for. My joy was complete when the passengers, including my husband, were all safe on board the Kong Halfdan.

All those who had gone ashore went expressly to visit a camp of Lapps, which was about a mile from the landing. The people were very much surprised to have so many strangers come upon them suddenly, so the children and dogs—and there were many of them—were badly scared; but the grown people seemed willing to stand and look. I missed seeing the camp by remaining back, but I saw many of the Lapps, for they hung about the ship's landing. They were a curiosity to us, for their dress was very odd,

Lapp Hut.

which you can see for yourselves by looking at the family in the picture. There is father, mother and six children, That seems to be a large family for such a small hut, but the Lapps live very close together, and the less house room there is, the less work the housewife has to do.

Those people are short in stature, measuring perhaps four or five feet in height. It is somewhat of a task to tell their complexion. Very little attention is paid to the care of it, but I'll say it seemed dark, rather copper-colored. If their faces were washed no doubt we should find a complexion altogether different from what has been described. The young Lapps have quite wrinkled, puckered-up looking faces, and with surprise you wonder why it is so. But when one takes into consideration the fact that most of their time is spent out of doors we cannot but conclude that wind and weather add nothing to their looks.

The Laplanders are an inoffensive class of people, we are told, and crimes among them are unknown; but they have a failing which I'm sorry to tell you of; it is that of strong drink. I have watched them pass into saloons; drunkenness is therefore no uncommon thing among them. What a dreadful habit to form; and men all over the world have given themselves over to the demon of strong drink, regardless of the consequences. I wish it were in my power to write something which would cause every boy who reads to keep far away from saloons. Look upon me as a friend, my boy readers, and let me ask you not to touch the vile stuff which is sold behind the screen. Remember that sadness and distress come to yourselves and families with the use of it. When tempted to drink do not, I beg of you, think it is manly to take a sip, and cowardly to refuse; but rather flee from the tempter and feel thankful you have escaped the fangs of the great serpent which seemed ready to fasten itself upon you. Ah, I hope you may never, never forget that death and destruction come with the use of strong drink! May the Lord stand by and save you from the evil!

Those who visited the camp at Tromsö were especially anxious to see their herd of reindeer; but the Lapps had already driven them to the mountains for pasture; so the people were too late. The reindeer eat everything green in their march to the mountains, and in the winter there is, far under the snow, a moss which they feed upon and are wonderfully quick in getting. They are a very useful animal to the Laplander, more so than horses are to us. The reindeer is harnessed to a sledge in winter and driven anywhere the Lapp desires to go. Three hundred pounds can be drawn by them, yet the amount is usually limited to a little over two hundred pounds.

These animals, as I said before, are quite useful, for the meat is used for food and the hide for clothing and shoes. They are milked, and butter and cheese are made from the milk. The milkmaid sometimes has a big time to get the milking done, for the reindeer doesn't want to stand still for her. You know some cows are not willing to be milked; they kick and move about too freely for the milkmaid's comfort. Well, the reindeer doesn't like milking time any better than the cow; and where there is a large herd to be milked it is necessary for a Lapp to get among them and throw a halter around the antlers, so that the animal may be held fast until milking is finished. You can imagine that man and maid have lively times while the catching is going on. Did you ever see the picture of a reindeer? Well, they have immense antlers, which come out from the head like great branches; and when the animal is full grown the antlers are very large, spreading far out and requiring a great deal of room. Where there is a herd of two or three hundred of them they have a big time among themselves hooking each other.

While on board the Kong Halfdan we had both salt and fresh reindeer meat, and liked it very much. If you were here now, I would show you a pair of Lapp shoes. The hide was tanned with the fur on, and in making the shoes the fur was left on the outside. They are odd looking and quite fanciful in their make-up.

Spoons and knife handles are made from the horns of the animal, and among our collection of Norway relics are two small spoons with a great deal of carving upon them, done by some of the Tromsö Lapps. I can't say the carving is fine at all, but it is rather amusing to look at.

Time passed rapidly away, and the eight hours' stop at Tromsö had ended. The passengers were all settled and the freight stored away. By and by the signal for starting was given; the ship turned about, and we steamed out of the bay. The atmosphere seemed quite cold at times, and we kept ourselves in our stateroom most of the time, sitting there wrapped in the steamer rug, passing the time in reading and writing to friends at home. The rocks and mountains kept us company, for from the porthole we saw them plainly. First they were to the right, then to the left of us.

One day when sitting in our stateroom the captain called to us and said, "Come up on deck and see Torghatten." Now, what do you think that was? Not one of you could guess, I'm sure, so I'll just tell you. Torghatten was a great high mountain with a hole through it. Right close to the top was a natural tunnel, and daylight could be seen through it plainly from where we stood. We looked in wonder at the great work of nature, and thought, "God can do anything." The earth, and all that is in it, was made by him; nothing is impossible with him. The forming of a hole in the top of a mountain is small compared to the many greater things he has done; and, dear children, will you think often of the Maker of this great universe? Will you keep in mind what power the Lord has? If so you will exclaim as I have many times, "How wonderful are thy works, O Lord!"

After passing Torghatten we continued standing on deck; and soon after we steamed past a great lot of rocks a mile or more wide. They were right out in the water and it seemed we would surely run on them with our big ship; but we didn't, though, and were glad of it too. On these rocks were hundreds of gray seagulls, and when the steamer went puffing along they all flew up with a cry of alarm, for they were badly scared. After finding we intended no harm they all came down again; and as we looked back we

The Hole in the Mountain.

could see them settling contentedly. You surely would have laughed if you had seen the scared seagulls.

Sometimes the ship stopped when far away from a station. We wondered why, but soon found that a light fog had settled around the ship. It comes down rather suddenly, and disappears just as suddenly as it comes. Often the bright sun is seen above, when all around the steamer is fog. The captain is compelled to stop his vessel and wait until the haze lifts. If he does not, there is great danger of running on the rocks, which are so plentiful that he must be cautious, or accidents will happen, and that would mean a loss of cargo, and lives too.

Along the coast of Norway are valuable mackerel, herring, lobster and cod fisheries. Several thousand men are employed, and the herring and cod are caught in immense quantities. Hundreds of pounds of herring and codfish are taken on at every station. The cod are dried and tied in large bundles. The herring are usually put down in brine and packed in barrels; many of them are dried, too, but it seemed that more were salted down. The people along the coast, as well as those living in the interior of Norway, eat a great many fish, for the lakes abound in the finest kind of them. The smallest fish, which are not salable, are fed to the hogs and chickens.

We had no trouble to get good fresh eggs to eat, for they were brought to the ship for sale. But at times they could not be eaten with a relish, as the taste of fish in them was too strong to make them palatable. That seemed to be a new revelation to us, and we decided that chickens ought not to be fed anything but the best of feed if an egg with a good taste is desired.

We saw fish everywhere: dried fish in the hold of the steamer, fish on the table cooked in many different ways, and live fish in the water; fish, fish, and no end to the different kinds. Fresh cod, trout and salmon were served on board the ship, and finer fish we never had the pleasure of eating. Several times cod liver was presented in our bill of fare. The seamen consider it a very fine dish. At first we ate but little of it; and I must say we never did like it as well as many other things upon the bill of fare.

We stopped to take on passengers and cargo at a small station. The day was clear and the sun shone beautifully. The people on shore were standing watching the loading of the ship and the boatmen were pulling at the oars, trying to get their little rowboats close to the side of the steamer; and I stood watching all, when my attention was suddenly drawn to the water, which was beautifully clear; so clear that I was able to see down, down many feet, and there in its depths I saw swimming with ease thousands of little codfish. The confusion above seemed not to frighten them in the least, for they came nearer and nearer the surface. The little fellows seemed hungry, so forthwith I procured a biscuit and fed it to them piece by piece. Thus I stood for an hour or more, feeding and watching them. How swift they were in their movements; for each little fish was bound to have a nibble. The one which came out victorious was compelled to eat his bite in a hurry, for there was no time to be lost. I am confident you would have enjoyed watching those fish, for it truly was a pleasant pastime.

After leaving the station we passed, to the left of us, a pile of rocks; and a waterfall seemed to be there too. Taking up the field glass we looked in the direction of the rocks, when, lo, nothing was to be seen but a daub of white paint a few feet long and perhaps a foot in width. Now what did that mean? Nothing but a trap by which to catch salmon. They are a hard fish to catch, and that invention was intended to lure them on to where nets were fixed to trap them. You see, the salmon desire fresh water, and they know it can only be found coming down from the mountain, so they swim for the supposed waterfall and are caught. The fishermen are quite ingenious; yet I always felt sorry for the poor fish.

Now do you know what that instance made me think of? Why, the evil one, who is continually setting traps for innocent children. Boys and girls, be careful you do not fall into the trap Satan sets for you. When you are tempted to tell an untruth, or to steal, or to play truant, or to be disobedient, just say, "I won't do it," and think that if you do any of these things you are getting into a trap which Satan has set to catch you.

Hammerfest was reached at last, and the captain said we might board on the Kong Halfdan and take trips to land whenever we desired to do so. It seemed strange indeed to be on land again, and no doubt the people thought so too, for they looked at us with amazement as we walked up one street and down another.

There were three or four little children who followed us from street to street, never saying a word. I asked them if they spoke English, but they gave no reply. We gave them a small piece of money, and they gave a look which told that they knew full well what money was. Dinner time came, still they followed, and I am very much afraid they lost their dinner that day.

I told you before that there were many fisheries along the coast. Well, this town seemed wonderfully fishy; there were warehouses in which were stored dried herring and codfish; then there were factories where cod-liver oil was made. You would be surprised to know how full the air was filled with the odor of cod-liver oil. We were told the smell was healthful, so we took it into our lungs more willingly; yet, if it had been possible for us to have a choice in the matter, we would gladly have had the air free from the odor, for surely it was very unpleasant.

Hammerfest is the farthest north of any town on the coast, and one day's journey from North Cape, the most northern point on the coast of Norway. The harbor at this place was full of vessels, both large and small, just as you see them in the picture, excepting two steamships which were then anchored far down in the bay. Spitzbergen is a great place for whalers and seal-hunters. It is four hundred miles from North Cape, the place where we had expected to go. History tells us that from this place several attempts have been made to reach the North Pole. Walruses, seals, foxes, reindeer, bears and birds are to be found there.

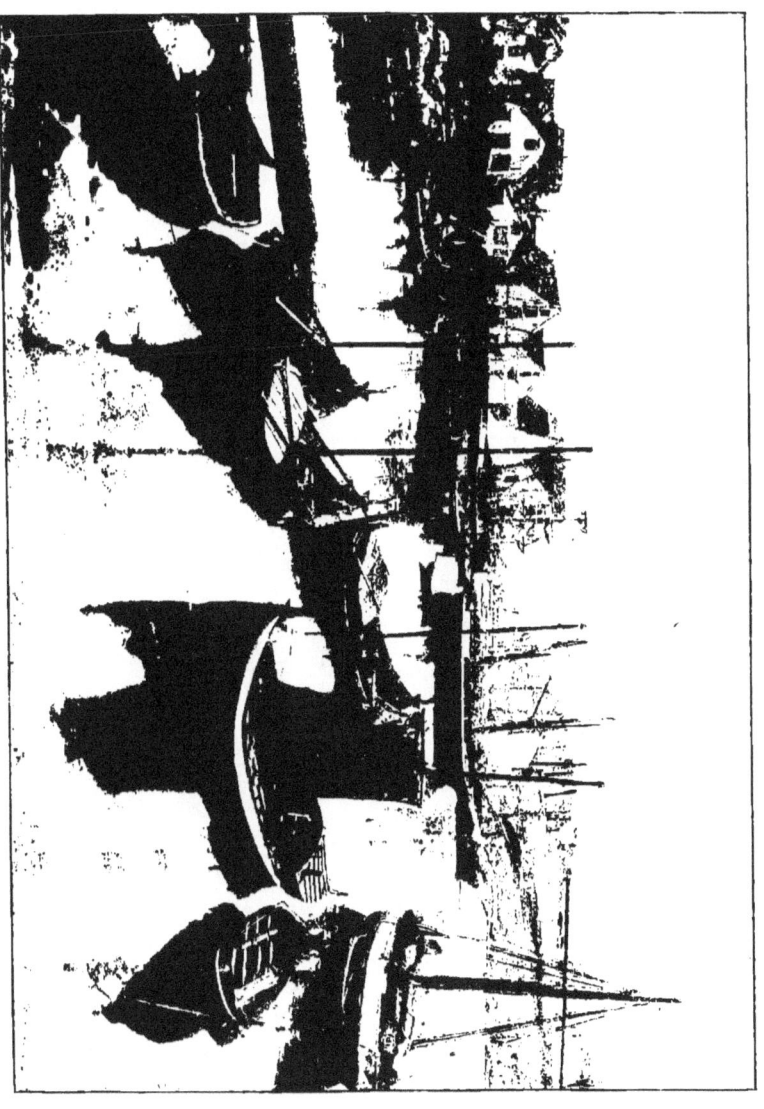

Hammerfest.

There was a vessel in from Spitzbergen which had been there only a few hours. As a rule she carried no passengers, but on the last trip one passenger had been taken aboard; and as there are no staterooms on sealing vessels, the passenger was given a box up on deck, and there, day and night, it stayed. The captain asked us if we would like to go over to the Spitzbergen ship and see the passenger. We said "Yes," so he had one of the Kong Halfdan's seamen take down a boat, and the captain rowed us out in the bay, over to where the ship was anchored. When we reached the vessel I thought I would just stand in the small rowboat and look over the sides; but the captain said, "Oh, but you must go on the sailing vessel, or you can't see all that is to be seen." Now there were no steps to go up, and no ladder to climb, so how could I get over? Well, seamen are used to climbing, and think everybody else is too; so he said, "Put one foot here, and the other up there, and then you will get up without trouble." I did as he directed, and in a little while I was on deck and looking around.

What did I see? Why, the hold of the ship packed full of fresh seal pelts. After killing the animals, they skinned them. The meat is thrown away, and the skins are taken to the hold of the ship, spread out, and salted right there. The next thing I saw was their passenger, and what do you think it was? A bear, a real live bear, and just fresh from the polar regions. It was about five months old, and just as white as white polar bears are.

The sailor who captured the bear said it fought nobly for freedom, and in the conflict he was unfortunate enough to have been bitten. The mother lost her life in the fight, and the hide hung near by to tell the story. In loud, pitiful tones the orphaned bear called for its mother; but no answer came back to it. I do not know where the cub found a home; but it was shipped to Throndhjem, and from there was to be sent to a museum. We were glad to leave the Spitzbergen ship and return to our own, for the mournful sound of the motherless white polar bear was not agreeable to us.

There had been a great fire in the town of Hammerfest, completely destroying the finest residences and best hotels just the winter before we reached there. It was thought the whole town would surely succumb and be burned to ashes. Our ship was the best hotel, and we were fortunate to get plenty to eat and a comfortable bed to sleep in. A change of quarters would have been pleasant if a good hotel could have been found; but as it was we were very well satisfied.

Hammerfest was the last stopping place along the line, and some of the sailors were off duty while the ship lay by at this place. About the first thing searched for is usually a saloon, and there is never any trouble to find one, for there are plenty of places where the poor fellows may find entertainment with cards and strong drink.

We had been on land a few hours and returned for luncheon, when our attention was attracted to a sailor upon the street who had indulged too freely in the use of whisky. He walked with unsteady gait to the ship landing, where eight or a dozen steps led to the boats in the water below.

No one could reach the steamer without descending the stairway and going in the rowboats; and we wondered how any person with such tottering steps could descend without falling into the water. So we watched, and he went down step by step stumbling, yet catching himself again and again. His comrades saw him, and taking one of the ship's boats rowed for the drunken sailor, reaching him just as his weakened knees gave way. Headlong he pitched into the boat, and with a splash his feet went into the water. That was a trying time for the boatman, but he seemed equal to the occasion, and by tugging and pulling succeeded in getting the poor fellow into the boat, feet and all. With a steady row and in silence the side of the steamer was gained, and with plenty of help the unfortunate one was pulled through a small door in the side of the ship. He disappeared, and nothing more was seen of him till the next day, when, rather long faced, he was seen on duty.

Now, children, you may be amused while reading this little incident of a drunken sailor, but just let me tell you that I was disgusted, and thought of the words of Solomon when he said, "Wine is a mocker, strong drink is raging: and whosoever is deceived thereby is not wise." The drunken sailor knew not what he was doing, and was unwise when he partook of strong drink. Now, boys, I'll give you something to learn, and as long as you shall live, don't ever forget it: "Woe unto them that rise up early in the morning, that they may follow strong drink; that continue until night, till wine inflame them!" "Who hath woe? who hath sorrow? who hath contentions? who hath babblings? who hath wounds without cause? who hath redness of eyes? They that tarry long at the wine; they that go to seek mixed wine. Look not thou upon the wine when it is red, when it giveth his color in the cup, when it moveth itself aright. At the last it biteth like a serpent, and stingeth like an adder. My son, give me thine heart, and let thine eyes observe my ways."

May the Lord bless you, boys, and keep you from the drunkard's cup.

There was nothing of great importance to be seen in Hammerfest, so we decided to make the return trip on the same steamer, which would leave after the cargo had been discharged. August twenty-sixth the anchor was hauled in and we started.

There was a little change in the return route, which gave us a sail of a day or so on the Arctic Ocean. We had not gone far till the wind rose, and we had what the captain called an "Arctic storm." The steamer was small, so it rolled and pitched a good deal. Oh how we wished to be out of that place! But one must put up with storms, and there is no use complaining about it either, for it does not help matters one bit, and a person is no happier.

There was a whaling station on the route, and the captain showed his kindness by telling some of the passengers that if they were so minded they could visit the camp. When my husband and a young German decided to go, the captain ordered the sailors to take a ship's boat and row them there and back again. The sea was very rough, so I decided to remain where I was, and not venture in a boat smaller than the Kong Halfdan.

It was thought by the men that I had acted wisely in not accompanying them. The camp was found in a miserably dirty condition, for whales in different stages of decomposition were seen all around it. The fat of the decayed animals was thrown into a vat and rendered just as we render the fat of a hog. Very large vats of boiling oil were to be seen, and the odor sickened those who were not used to it; and I'm sure it would have sickened me too.

For three days the weather was unpleasant, and a good share of that time I stayed in my stateroom. A great deal of rain falls in Norway during the summer, and it is quite necessary to carry rain-cloaks and a rubber blanket to throw over the baggage. These things are more needful to those traveling on land, because they are more exposed to the weather than persons who travel on water. We were well supplied with the necessary wraps, yet had but little use for them.

Sunday was the fifth day on the return trip, and the sun came out bright and clear. Even though it was Sunday the sailors worked faithfully taking on and off freight. We made a stop at a little village whose houses extended down to the water. A little white church, with green grass around it, looked so cozy standing in the beautiful sunlight. The bells were ringing and the sound came over the water to us. What a cheerful sound! and it created a desire within us to go and worship with the gathering congregation. We could not go ashore, for the steamer might leave us behind; and that would never do. Many barrels of herring were taken aboard that day, and four hours passed before we steamed away; plenty of time to have gone ashore had we known it; but the privilege of mingling our prayers with those of the little congregation had passed away forever.

Our ship was heavily laden with salted and dried fish, besides several hundred barrels of whale oil. All deck room was taken up, and only a narrow space was left us to walk upon. Passengers got on and every stateroom was occupied; besides many beds were made up in the dining saloon, and we were pretty well crowded.

We found the Kong Halfdan was not in very good repair, for there seemed to be a good deal of tinkering done to the boiler; day and night, by spells, we heard the hammering. Upon inquiry we found the boiler had been leaking, and that it was not an easy matter to patch it up. When the sea washed the deck, or a hard rain came, the water dripped down in our stateroom, splashing dirty water on such articles as were near. Time did not pass any too swiftly for us, and we were glad to know that only a few days more and our feet would be on mother earth again.

The scenery was grand all along the route, but the bad condition of the ship kept us from enjoying it to the fullest extent. You must surely know it is not a pleasant thought to be in a position where you are unable to help yourself if an accident should happen. It is not best to borrow trouble; yet there are times when it seems impossible to keep from doing so.

One morning about six o'clock we were awakened from a sound sleep by a peculiar grating noise. The steamer had struck a reef of rocks, and I shall never forget the sensation. With one bound we were out of our berths, and, with but few words passing between us, dressed hastily. We knew full well that if a hole had been broken in the ship, with such a heavy cargo only a short time could pass before she would sink. Upon examination it was found that the propeller was injured, but not badly. In a few days after we steamed into Throndhjem Bay safely, and our hearts were filled with gratitude to the Lord for his watchful care. We were glad to have an opportunity to see so much of nature, for by it many good sermons were preached to us, and these words filled our mind, "O Lord, how great are thy works; and thy thoughts are very deep."

CHAPTER IV.

The Story of a German Boy.—The Priest.—Catholic Woman.—Corps of Singers. — My Singing Lesson. — Funeral Procession. — Children Playing.— Wooden Shoes. — Neatness of the German Children.— Their Politeness.—Cologne.—Its Cathedral.— Height of Towers.— Odd Costumes.—Art Gallery.—The Picture I Saw.

AM going to tell you something about Germany now, but will first tell you of a boy who lived there many years ago. He had father, mother, brothers and sisters, and as a family they were very poor. The father worked hard in the copper mines, along with many other men in the settlement, and at home the mother worked equally hard looking after the comfort of the family and carrying upon her back the wood which was needed. She was a good, kind, Christian mother, and it is said she frequently "communed with God in prayer."

Those times everybody belonged to the Roman Catholic church; consequently every father and mother taught the children to believe fully—as they themselves did—in the "Holy Catholic Church." This boy was the eldest of the family and was the first to be educated. As he neared the age when it would be necessary to send him away to school the parents became anxious. They knew they could ill afford to do it, as they had scarcely money enough for their daily need and no chance of getting more. There seemed to be one way in which they might be enabled to save a little more money, and that was by living still more economically; and by putting their thoughts into practice enough money was saved to give the son a start in school. Not many miles distant from the boy's home was a select school, and thither the father and son went shortly after money enough had been saved. The support which his father gave him was not sufficient to cover expenses, so the lad was finally obliged to help himself, which was done by singing from door to door. As a reward small pieces of money were given him. The strictest economy was practiced by the folks at home and the son also, and as a reward for all their trouble they learned that the boy for whom they were making those sacrifices was studious and worked hard and faithfully.

Time rolled on, the boy had grown to manhood and become a great teacher. He seemed strong in the Romish faith and willing to make sacrifices for his church. By and by the duty of becoming a priest or monk was impressed upon him, and as soon as possible he wrote his intentions to his father. The reply to the letter was not favorable. As the new move was very displeasing to the parents, they said that if such a step should be taken further affection would be renounced. Those words availed nothing, for the vow was taken and the young priest was received into the order with prayers and hymns of joy.

As the priest grew older his work in the church increased, and that caused him to read and study the Bible more diligently, and in so doing he found he was not serving the Lord fully.

Years passed away, and the young priest became dissatisfied with his religion and decided to follow what he found to be the teachings of the Bible. In the course of time, and after much trouble, he separated himself from the Romish church, and from that time on his life was in great danger, for the Catholics were very bitter toward him. The Lord is thoughtful of his children, so he watched over this good man and allowed him to live many years after.

Now whom do you imagine I've been writing about? Well, I shall tell you. It was Martin Luther, the founder of the state church of Germany, which is known throughout the world as the Lutheran church; and now almost everybody in Germany belongs to the state church, and not the Catholic church, as in the time of Martin Luther. This man's name is held high above all and his portrait is to be seen in almost every German home. Many of the beautiful churches which were owned by the Catholics are now used and owned by the Lutherans.

One day while out walking with a Catholic woman we passed a large cathedral, and with trembling voice she said, "This belonged to our people one time, but it is ours no more." I felt sorry, and thought, "No wonder your heart is sad, for surely your house of worship is a very poor one compared to this;" for it was in a back street and dark and gloomy looking. The woman had nothing to feel proud of, therefore lamented.

We happened to be in Germany on the four hundredth anniversary of Luther's birthday, and a big day it was; there were processions and illuminations all over the city. The house in which Luther lived while in Halle was finely decorated with evergreen, and the gas jets were beautiful. It was not hard to tell where Catholics lived, for their houses alone were without lights. It was plain to be seen that no one stands higher in the minds of the people than Martin Luther.

Many of the students attending college in Germany make part of their expenses as did Martin Luther, by singing from door to door. Their voices are well trained, and when a square or two from them, the whole company of voices seemed like four voices, their singing accorded so well. The corps of singers is composed of a dozen or more young men, and though their size varies their dress is alike, for they wear black suits of clothing; the vest is cut low, exposing the shirt bosom; the coat is cut swallow-tail, and upon the head a plug hat is worn. Their ages range from twelve to sixteen years, and you may imagine how very odd the company looked to us. There is a leader who stands before them beating time, and I don't believe any one of them miscalculates the length of a note or rest in the piece of music sung. I am sure many of you never heard finer singing.

Germans, as a rule, are fine singers, and you hear plenty of singing even while walking upon the streets. One time we were awakened from a sound sleep by singing on the street. We looked out of the window and beheld a company of soldiers all singing as they marched along. Little boys and girls go home from school, walking along leisurely and singing beautiful hymns and songs.

We were living with a family who had several children, and one of them, a little girl about seven years of age, dearly loved to sing. This little girl insisted upon my helping her, but I said, "I cannot sing in German," when immediately she replied, "I will teach you my tune." The task was begun, and after a great deal of laughing and many corrections I was able to sing her hymn, "*Stille Nacht*" (Stilly Night). Quickly she ran to her mother and told the news, and I was congratulated, for the family thought I had done a wonderful thing. To tell the truth, I was equally well pleased, and afterward took pleasure in singing my German hymn.

You may think, by the way I have been writing, that everything in the old world moves along pleasantly, and that the children are always well and happy. I would not have you think so, because sorrow and distress are there, as well as in this country.

In looking out of my window, which was quite often, I saw that which was amusing, and also some things which were very sad. One day a funeral procession passed by, and it consisted of father and mother. Four pall bearers carried a casket containing the corpse of a little child. The rain came down fast, and equally fast fell the tears of sorrow from their eyes as slowly they moved along. There was no hearse, and no carriages. Why? Because the people were poor; it would take money for these things, and there was none to spare. Ah, how my heart ached for them, and I turned from my window with tearful eyes. Poverty is to be found on all sides, and since it is impossible to help all we learn to cast the distressing sights from our minds and leave them with the One who watches over and cares for all.

An American is surprised at the cleanliness of German cities. It is no uncommon sight to see well-dressed ladies walking in the middle of the streets. Their shoes and skirts will not be soiled any quicker by walking there than on the sidewalk. We feel ashamed when we compare the dirty streets of American cities with the clean, well-swept streets of Germany, and in our hearts we wished ours might be different.

Houses are built three stories high; each floor is arranged for one family, but sometimes there are as many as three families living on one floor, each having no more than one room in which to sleep, cook, eat and sit. I knew a family of five who lived in one room; and they seemed to be well satisfied too.

No matter where one goes he is sure to see many children, and they seem to have as good a time playing as any of you. They run, jump and make as much noise too. Many times I stood at my window in Halle and watched the little folks play on the opposite side of the street. One time I counted fifteen boys and girls playing, and their ages seemed to be from five to ten years; and—don't you think?—they all belonged to the same house. Now you might think their little feet pattering on the floor would make a great noise, but they don't, because all wear felt slippers in the house; even the fathers and mothers wear them. In Germany the floors are not carpeted as in this country, but almost all of them are bare. Where families are in good circumstances nice rugs are used; where there are no rugs the floors are sanded, and you can't imagine how strange it does seem to walk on sanded floors. Felt slippers are fine things to keep the feet warm, and I know the little folks over there would have cold toes all the time if it were not for those comfortable slippers.

Wooden shoes and slippers are worn quite a good deal, and many times I laughed heartily when the little boys and girls ran. No matter whether I was looking out of the window or sitting back in the room, I could always tell when they had commenced their running. Do you wonder how I knew it? Why, just by the noise they made. I presume many of you never saw a pair of wooden shoes or slippers. Well, that doesn't make any difference, for I never saw a pair until I went to the Old Country,—I have learned since then that there are plenty of wooden shoes in America, and not so many miles from where I am living. There is a difference between shoes and slippers. Just take one of your old shoes, tear off the leather excepting the part that covers the toes, then substitute a wooden sole instead of a leather one, and you can imagine how they look. You would naturally suppose it to be quite a task to keep such a foot covering on when running; but you will be surprised to know they did not seem one bit bothered, and I am pretty sure the German children can run just as fast as any of you. Sometimes they stop to shove their toes farther into the slipper, after which they run as fast as ever. And now why did I laugh? Because of the great noise all the little wooden slippers made. What made them make a noise? Why, the sole of the slipper flying up and down. At regular intervals you could hear a noise that sounded like clap, clap, clap, and the faster the children ran the more clap, claps we could hear; somehow this was always very amusing to me.

Many of the Germans are poor; yes, very poor; and yet,—don't you know?—with all their poverty, the children's clothing never looked ragged. Their clothing is sometimes made of very coarse material, and often many patches are to be seen, but no tatters. They all wore woolen stockings, knit by hand; not one time did I see the bare heel of a child sticking out. All stockings were well darned. Could not some of our American mothers learn lessons of carefulness and economy from these poor German women?

Let me tell you something, little girls. You who are old enough to read are old enough to do a little sewing too, and how nice it would be for you to take hold and learn now! Long years ago I was a little girl; one time,—when ten years old,—my sister said, "Lizzie, when a tiny little hole comes in your stocking, it is a good plan to darn it right away; then you will never have to darn a great big hole, which seems so trying to the patience." The advice was good, and I followed it accordingly; to this day I have never felt sorry for the advice of long ago. Will you think of it too, little girls?

Children in the Old Country are taught to be very polite. It made no difference where they saw us, a bow and "*Guten Morgen*" (Good morning) was the greeting. Even though we did not know the names of the little girls and boys, it seems they knew us, having learned to know we lived on the same street they did. Don't you think it is a good thing to be polite? I wonder why little folks here act rude and pass by those who speak to them, acting as though they never knew the gentleman or lady who spoke? Perhaps teachers and parents forget to teach the little ones politeness.

Writing about poverty brings to my mind the little boys and girls who ate bread spread with lard instead of butter. And now I wonder how many of you, my little readers, would enjoy that kind of fare. No doubt you will say, "Oh, how horrid;" but let me tell you that those children ate their bread with a relish, and maybe you would too if you knew there was nothing better for you. They learned to know almost everything tastes good when one is hungry.

The Old World is full of relics of the past, and there is scarcely a city that does not have a church, art gallery or museum in which one might spend much time and be greatly edified.

We spent several days in Cologne, and by hiring a carriage for a couple of hours had a splendid opportunity of seeing the city, which is beautifully situated upon the left bank of the river Rhine. At one time a very thick wall surrounded the city and it was pierced with four gates. Only a small portion of wall attached to the gates is to be seen now, for the rest has been removed. Outside of the old gateways there are beautiful residences, and great pains are taken to beautify the front dooryards. The streets in the old part of the city are crooked, narrow and not very clean looking, but in the new portion they are quite the reverse.

Cologne is an old city, and there are many very old churches which we found to be interesting, not only because of their age, but because of the works of art; for these are paintings which were done by the best painters the world knew. In this city is a fine church, or cathedral, which greatly attracts the attention of tourists, and many of them travel hundreds of miles just to see it, and it alone. It is a very large structure, therefore has had many, many years of work put upon it; even while we were looking around the workmen were busily engaged in hammering. The cathedral is built in the form of a cross and is said to be four hundred and eighty feet long, two hundred and eighty-two feet wide, and the height of the central aisle one hundred and fifty-four feet. Just notice in the picture how far above the houses the towers extend. Well, when they are completed their height will be upwards of five hundred feet. There is a chime of bells, six in number, up in the tower, and the heaviest of the bells weighs eleven tons. With that chime music was made, and it was such a pleasure to sit in my room, which was not far away, and listen to the beautiful tunes as they were played one by one. The windows in the *Dom Kirche*—for it is known by that name—were all presented at different times, and are richly colored, each one representing some Bible character, the Virgin Mary being the central figure in some of them. For the sum of one and a half marks each we were admitted into the treasury where were stored many costly things, such as jewels, gold and silver ornaments and many other things of great value. The high choir and chapel were not open to visitors free, but after high mass was celebrated those who visited the treasury were allowed to see all the rest. But I shall not write any longer on this subject, for possibly you may tire of it.

In traveling through Germany we noticed in certain localities that the women wore very odd looking costumes. The skirts were extremely full, and in length reached the knee. Some wore very long white stockings, and others wore black ones, all wearing very low slippers. The hair was combed up on the very top of the head, and for a bonnet a sort of a box was worn, just large enough to cover the top of the head and hair. They were the most oddly dressed women we ever did see, and—don't you know?—they did not attract extra attention from the passers-by. No doubt this way of dressing had been handed down from generation to generation; therefore everybody living in that locality was used to it.

The Germans are great people for pictures, oil paintings, etc., and works of the great masters are to be seen in

Cathedral at Cologne.

their galleries. One could spend hours wandering from gallery to gallery, studying the paintings one by one; for the more we look at fine pieces of art the more we admire them. Not only do we admire the man who did the work, but through him think of the Divine Hand which gave the mind to the great artist.

While in Munich, a large city in Germany, we visited a gallery of very fine paintings. Among those in which we were particularly interested was an immense painting of the judgment day. There, seated in a chair, was the judge, and in the foreground were to be seen graves, some opening and others already open. Both men and women were to be seen coming forth, and as they stepped from their graves they started for the judge; and they soon found on which side they belonged. Only a few were to be seen sitting on the right side, and the rest disappeared with faces ghastly and full of distress; and those who were seated on the right side of the judge had faces beaming with pleasure. While looking at this work of art I could not help but call to mind the portion of Scripture which says, "Depart from me, I never knew you," etc. The painting was to represent the Son of Man sitting upon the throne and judging all the nations of the earth. It was only a picture and work of man, but it was good enough to make an impression on my mind, for it caused me to think of the distress which awaits all who do not do the Lord's bidding, and so are unprofitable servants. I have found it pays to be a true follower of Christ, for there is joy unspeakable in serving him. I hope you will think seriously of the salvation of your souls. Be lambs in the fold of Christ, so that you may have the happy privilege of being seated at the right hand of the great Judge on the last day.

CHAPTER V.

Calais. — English Channel Experience. — Reaching the Pier. — Going Ashore. — London. — The Fog.—Show Lights.—British Museum.— National Gallery.—The Tricky Monkey.—Westminster Abbey.—The Tower.

THE next point of interest to be visited was London, England; so early one morning we took the train at Cologne, traveled all day, and arrived after dark at Calais, a town of France. At this point we left the railway and went aboard the steamer which conveys passengers and mail across the Channel to Dover, a distance of perhaps twenty-six miles.

There is a fine harbor at Calais, but owing to the darkness of the night we were not able to see it then. There was not a moment of time to lose, for the steamer was ready to start back on her return trip to Dover. There were but few passengers on board that evening, and down deep in my heart I wished we had been among the number who had wisdom enough to remain on shore. But one is not always able to see the danger which may be ahead, and must therefore suffer the consequences.

As soon as the steamer left the harbor we felt very sure a trying time was in store for us; but it was too late to turn back, so we tried to make the best of the situation by making ourselves comfortable. The English Channel is affected very much by storms on the coasts, and at such times the waters become greatly troubled; so much so that ships are wrecked and many lives lost. On this particular day a very severe storm raged; it had started on the Irish coast and by the time the Channel was reached there was a genuine cyclone. The wind blew a gale and the breakers dashed against the steamer until the little thing rolled and pitched shockingly. Truly we were in dangerous waters, and we were made to feel it more keenly after hearing an order given to the sailors to "take down the life-buoys." Never before in our journeyings by sea had such an order been given in our hearing; so you may believe it made me sick at heart. Seasickness did not trouble us, strange to say, though the steward came to us often, thinking perhaps we should need assistance; but there was nothing needed excepting a quiet sea. Each time the man came around husband asked, "How are we getting along now? Shall we soon be over?" and the reply came, "This is a very bad night, sir; but we hope to make the pier."

Seasickness would have been a small thing to endure compared to the distress which followed, for by this time my nerves were unstrung and I was in agony. Nothing could be done but bear the distress, and silently I groaned prayer after prayer to the Father above. Very few were my words, for I remembered the Lord did not hear us alone for our much speaking, and in such a perilous situation one does not stop to choose the words he may utter. Again and again I groaned, "O Lord, keep thy watchful eye upon us; and I pray thee keep thy children from the dangers of this angry sea." We placed ourselves in the hands of the Lord, and oh what a feeling of security there was; and in the words of the Psalmist we were able to say, "The Lord, he is my refuge and my fortress: my God, in him will I trust." Yes, even though our bodies trembled, our hearts were strong in him, and we trusted. The Lord had been especially good to us, not because we were deserving, but perhaps because he wanted us a little longer on the earth that his servant—my husband—might have a longer time in which to tell of the "truths of God's Word."

We read that "they that seek the Lord shall not want any good thing," and in my Christian experience I have found the blessings were beyond my hope. "Come, ye children, hearken unto me: I will teach you the fear of the Lord." He desires boys and girls in his kingdom. Will you seek him early? Remember Samuel; he was but a child when he "ministered before the Lord." And then think of Daniel; what a good young man he was, for we read that he had an excellent spirit and "he was faithful; neither was there any error or fault found in him." That was a good recommendation; but we learn more about him; he prayed, and was not ashamed of it either; for we read of a decree which had been signed by king Darius and sent out. It said, "Whosoever shall ask a petition of any god or man for thirty days, save of thee, O king, he shall be cast into the den of lions." Daniel no doubt felt badly when he heard of the decree; but nevertheless he went three times a day and prayed as had been his custom. The result you know.

My young readers, do you want good examples of Christians? then pattern after these boys of whom I have written. The Lord watched over them; he delivered Daniel from the lion's den into which he had been cast for praying. Do you know he will help you to bear the scoffs and jeers of your comrades if you should forsake them and follow him? You know "Jesus said unto Simon, Fear not"? And to you he says the same. Will you think of these things?

In thinking over the experience on the Channel I call to mind a sound which, though far away, proved to be soothing in its effect. I imagine you say, What was it? So I'll tell you that while lying upon my couch that night I heard a sailor off in a distant part of the steamer hurrying around performing his duties; and while doing so he whistled in a cheery, joyful tone. The waves were breaking high then, and perhaps the sailor never thought the sound would reach the ears of any one except his comrades who were rushing around near by him. But a current of wind brought the music to me. and from now till I leave this world I shall never forget that whistling. For a few minutes self was forgotten and my nerves quieted, and then there came an end to the whistling, for a voice called loudly, "She is fast;" and that meant the pier had been gained. But joy did not come then, for the next thing we knew we were steaming out to sea again, rolling and pitching as hard as ever.

Twice the attempt was made to gain the landing, but each time the heavy breakers washed the vessel away. The third attempt was made and success crowned the effort, when immediately after came the order, "Make haste and go ashore." This order was given to the passengers, and as soon as possible we all undertook the difficult task of getting to the passageway which led to land. The breakers dashed furiously over the side of the steamer and great banks of water poured down upon our heads and backs, for we stood still with faces turned from the direction of the breaking waves. We scarcely knew how to reach shore without help, for the water came with a dash at regular intervals, making it almost impossible for us to walk. Thinking the sailor might assist us in landing I ventured to ask him, saying, "Oh, will you not help us over the passageway?" but the answer came, "No, madam, I dare not." There was nothing to hinder him from helping us while upon the boat, so taking my hand we hurried along over the deck until the inclined passageway was gained, when he left me to stumble on in the dark. Rain cloaks were of little service that night, for the salt sea water went through them, and consequently the clothing was dripping wet.

Land was gained at last, and immediately we entered the cars which were waiting to carry passengers and mail on to London. After getting our breath we looked around, and to our utter surprise found that the seats and floor had been drenched with water which had entered through the windows, which had been broken by the waves dashing against them while the cars were standing upon the pier. The admiralty pier is a massive structure extending out into the sea; and during the storm some of the immense stones were washed out and carried away. Papers of the following day gave full accounts of the storm, and the record of shipwrecks was enormous. It is said the like of such a storm had not been known for many, many years. I think the memory of it will abide with me while life shall last, and I shall always feel that the Lord watched over us and heard our prayers.

Twelve o'clock that night we reached the great city of London, and it was in a drenching rain. We were taken to a hotel a long distance from the depot, which place we called home for three weeks. When my health allowed me, I accompanied my husband to places of interest, but there were very many days when I was not able to bear the noise upon the streets, so remained within the cheerless hotel room. All large cities are cheerless and disagreeable in rainy weather; but it seemed to me the city of London was the most disagreeable one of all, for there was a great deal of rain and much foggy weather at that time. The fog becomes very dense sometimes, and those times it is quite dangerous to be upon the streets. The city is well lighted, and yet when the fog comes down the lights seem to be of but little use. Teamsters call out, "Show lights! show lights!" and as soon as possible the people place lights in every window of their houses. People who are out walking are unable to know when a horse is near them, and no doubt many are trampled under the horses' feet.

We visited many places of great interest while in this large city, and though I shall not be able to tell of all the attractive objects seen I will briefly mention a few of them. The British Museum was only a few blocks from our hotel, so much of our time was spent there looking at the relics which had been collected from all parts of the world.

There is a "National Gallery" in London, and there you find paintings of noted artists on exhibition. Almost every day in the week it is open to the public free; so a great many people spend hours looking at the beautiful work of man, which is done either with pencil or brush. Many of the old artists took much pleasure in painting the "Madonna and· Child," and that means Mary and Jesus; and in almost every instance the face of the mother is wonderfully beautiful; the child is plump in body and has a round, full face. Joseph and his brethren, John the Baptist, and other Bible characters were there, for it seems that noted artists of long ago spent their time in putting on canvas what they imagined the saints of old looked like; and most of them are represented as being fine looking men.

It is impossible for me to write you a description of all the interesting pieces of art on exhibition there, so we shall leave the Gallery and visit the Zoological Gardens, for it seemed to be an attractive place for old and young people. Animals of all countries may be seen there, and who is it that does not desire to see animals of foreign lands? We spent one afternoon there, and in our wanderings saw the rhinoceros and hippopotamus — both natives of Africa. Then there were the great, clumsy looking elephants, some of which were allowed to walk about without chains. One of them had a large platform fixed upon his back, and for a certain sum of money any one who desired could have a ride up one avenue and down another. There was a man to lead the animal, and you would be surprised to know how many boys, girls and middle-aged people took the ride. We watched them, but got no closer.

Children enjoy looking at monkeys, and on the afternoon we were at the Gardens there were numbers of them at the monkey cages throwing in crackers, apples and cakes; and oh how the little folks laughed when a monkey hung by his tail from the perch, or undertook the task of scratching his neighbor's head. They are wonderfully tricky; so every one is cautioned to keep away from the cages, to not get too close to the wires. Here and there were printed cards which said, "Persons with spectacles keep away." You see the monkeys had a habit of snatching off the glasses, and that accounted for the warning.

A young girl with her lover stood close to the cage that afternoon. She was decked in the height of style, with an immense bunch of flowers upon her hat; and over her face was a thin vail. One of the tricky fellows quick jumped up, ran his thin paws out between the wires and in an instant had the little face vail in his paws; and jumping on the perch sat there and tore it in shreds, while occasionally shy glances were cast at the young girl whose crimson face told of the embarrassment felt, for all eyes were upon her. Every one around laughed, and the children could hardly forget the cunning little monkey.

If one of these little fellows saw you put your hand in your pocket, he was sure you would bring out something for him; and if you gave him nothing there was a look of disappointment.

The lions, tigers and hyenas were visited next, and we found them growling, and prancing back and forth. It was feeding time, and the keeper gave them great chunks of raw meat, which they devoured ravenously. But evening was drawing near, so we left there and went to our hotel, reaching there in time for dinner,—the evening meal.

Westminster Abbey is a church, and it is a sacred place for the English people, for in it are to be seen the tombs of kings, queens and other noted people. In looking around one is impressed with the thought of age; and no wonder, for we read that the Abbey had been destroyed by the Danes, and re-erected by King Edgar in the year 985. But it seems to have been "entirely rebuilt in the latter half of the 13th century by Henry the Third and his son Edward the Fifth, who left it substantially in its present condition." The Abbey seems almost like a graveyard, for as you pass up one aisle and down another you behold large monuments erected in memory of noble men who fell in battle.

How strange it seemed to be standing by the tombs of kings and queens of whom we had read when school children. There in a vault were the remains of Charles the Second, William the Third, and Queen Mary his wife. And further on was the monument of Queen Elizabeth. I might go on and write many pages of what we saw there, but must leave the gloomy, dismal place. I wondered how people could worship in a place where there is such a grand display of monuments and tombs.

The Tower of London is said to be the most interesting spot in England. It is found outside of the bounds of the ancient city walls. It has four entrances,—the "Iron Gate, the Water Gate, and the Traitor's Gate." These gates are on the side next to the river Thames. The men who act as guards are called "Wardens or Beef-eaters." I think every one of them is a very old man. The strange term beef-eater is explained as being "a nickname bestowed upon the ancient yeomen of the guard from the fact that rations of beef were regularly served out to them when on duty."

In the Tower is the armory, where may be seen implements of war and torture, figures of horses almost as natural looking as life, and soldiers seated upon their backs equipped for war; a good representation of how the warriors of the time of king Charles First and William the Conqueror looked when ready for fight. There we saw the beheading block, axe and mask which were used in the dreadful work of sending people into eternity.

There is a chapel which no visitors are allowed to enter, and in it are buried celebrated persons who were beheaded. In the year 1535 the first person was executed, and in the following year, 1536, Queen Anne Boleyn was beheaded upon the green; and we stood near the spot where the bloody deed was done, for a marble slab marks the place. When looking at the beheading block we could not help but think of the untold agony it could tell were it but able to speak. Many noted people, both men and women, were at different times imprisoned in the Tower, placed there to await the time of execution. But sometimes one of them would be murdered there, while others again were tortured and then taken away to be burned as heretics. Those were distressing times, and innocent people suffered.

There are on exhibition in the Tower the crown of Queen Victoria and many solid gold vessels. Among the collection were beautiful golden saltcellars. One of them was made in imitation of a large castle and is beautifully studded with precious stones. There were staffs and scepters which sparkled with diamonds as they lay in the sunlight. Policemen guarded well the case which contained them, for not every person is honest who looks at them, and attempts have been made to break through the case.

Days seemed to go by rapidly, and three times Sunday came while we were in London. It was usually a quiet day for a city, as only a few teams passed on the street in front of our hotel. 'Bus horses had a season of rest then, for they run on half time. Stores were closed, and even the hotel employees had rest, for only two meals were allowed the guests. The whole city had a restful air which made one think the most of the inhabitants had gone to some place of worship.

There is a house of worship called the "Temple Church," and Dr. Parker is the minister; so we decided to go to hear him. The church was crowded with people, for it proved to be the day of their harvest home meeting,—something entirely new to us. We were favored with a good seat and not far from the stand where the learned doctor stood. Upon this rostrum was a mass of flowers, fruits, vegetables and bread, all arranged tastefully; yet they did seem to be very much out of place in a church. However, we overlooked that when we found that each article there was a free-will offering for the poor and sick, given by any one, and presented to those who were in need of them. Sick people were the recipients of flowers, and the bread and vegetables went to the poor and destitute.

At the close of our harvests we sometimes gather together and have a harvest meeting; but we are not thoughtful enough to bring an offering of the fruit of our land, as did the English people. If we are blessed with an abundance would it not be well to divide with less favored ones?

Well, Dr. Parker preached an excellent sermon, and his prayer was so comforting. Willingly would we have remained longer in the church, but that was out of the question; so we passed out with the crowd into the street, and to the place we tried hard to call home. Each Sunday some place of worship was attended, but we rather preferred Dr. Parker to any other minister.

Time seemed to pass rapidly away, and by and by we bade adieu to London, crossed over the Channel and found ourselves safe in France. The English Channel was rather smooth and the steamer crowded with passengers who had been waiting for the storm to cease. The passage was delightful, and I enjoyed the trip as much as a person with shattered nerves might expect to enjoy it. After riding in the cars three or four hours we reached the city of Paris, and that you know is the capital of France, and a very large city. We were there four weeks. Each day we visited places of interest, such as public buildings, palaces and cathedrals, public squares and cemeteries. Of the last named there is one called Pere la Chaise. It contains one hundred and six and a half acres. It is laid out in avenues and seems almost like a city, with its grand tombs, large enough to hold many, many people. We noticed that illustrious personages were buried there, for we saw the names of lords and ladies. Poor people were not able to buy lots there, so were content to place their dead in less beautiful places. It is the custom in Paris for persons to take off their hats on meeting a funeral procession, whether in the country or in the public streets. That seemed like an odd custom, but one gets used to many strange sights when abroad.

The sewers of Paris are spoken of very highly, and it is said they are four hundred and forty-one miles in length. Some of the sewers are wide enough to allow boats to pass through them, and at certain times of the year visitors may take a tour through them; but they must first have a special permit. The river Seine flows through Paris, and small excursion steamboats take passengers out, thus giving a good view of both sides of the river and landing them at small towns outside of the city limit.

There is no use for me to try to tell you all we saw in Paris, for each day there were new sights presented to us.

Seeing the fashions seems to be the highest ambition of some people, and many of them go to Paris for that purpose. People are able to gratify the desire there, and it is to be hoped they return home satisfied.

CHAPTER VI.

Venice.—A Gondola.—The Pigeons.—Trieste.—Piræus.—Athens.—Paul and Mars' Hill.—Sickness.—From Athens to Smyrna.—Man Overboard.—A Lesson of Unselfishness.—Smyrna.—A Cruel Father.—Ephesus.—Paul's Missionary Journey.—The Vesta.—Beyrut.—Jaffa Landing.

YOU may go with me, in your mind, to Venice, a city in Italy, where we found ourselves very early one winter morning. Day had not yet dawned, and darkness reigned supreme. Lamps were burning inside of the depot, giving just light enough for passengers to see every object plainly. At the foot of a flight of steps not far away stood two men, and as we were in search of a hotel porter we immediately walked toward them. Upon their cap-band, in large letters, was the name of the hotel we desired going to, and without speaking one word our traveling bags were taken and placed in a small boat, and we followed after, taking a seat near by them. We were strangers, ignorant of the language, cold and tired.

The boatmen dipped their oars with a splash, and in the mean time talked loudly to each other. The townspeople, no doubt, were in bed asleep, for not a sound but that of our boatmen was heard, and no lights were seen, excepting the lights which marked the corners. The distance seemed great, for we paddled up one canal and down another, until we knew not where the starting point was, and had no idea where the men were taking us.

Venice was the strangest city we had ever visited. Front doorsteps extended out into the water, and boatmen pulled up alongside of them with their little gondolas. A large door showed us the entrance to the hotel; but it was closed, and with a great deal of energy our fist came down against it. After patiently waiting, admittance was gained, for a winking, blinking-eyed servant, with hair standing straight up over his head, had heard the noise and appeared to find out the cause. In one hand he held a candle, and with the other kept tight hold of the door. At first thought an entrance seemed out of the question; but after his eyes were opened more widely he saw better and knew we were guests of the hotel; so forthwith the door opened and we passed into the hall, where a man who was not dazed took charge of us and we were glad to be taken to our room, where in a short time after we were warmly covered up in bed. Our journey had been long and tiresome, and the next morning found us still tired and not willing to rise early.

Venice was the meeting point for us, as a party of tourists, and from there we were to go on to Jerusalem together. We were ahead of time, so decided to go sight-seeing by ourselves; and an enjoyable time was had going from one point to another.

History tells us much about the city I'm writing about, but time and space will not allow me to repeat it to you.- I will, however, tell you that Venice is said to stand on one hundred and seventeen islands. There are one hundred and fifty canals, and those canals are spanned by three hundred and eighty bridges. There are a few narrow streets where people can walk, and when standing in the middle of one with arms outstretched, the walls of the houses on either side can easily be touched. There are also a few streets a little wider than the first named, but I must say only a very few.

Horses and wagons are never seen in the city, and the people who never go from home do not know what a horse looks like. Do you wonder how the people get along without horses and wagons? Well, they use little boats called gondolas. A gondola is long and narrow, with a flat bottom. One man rows it, using one oar, and always standing at the stern of his boat. He is called a gondolier. It is very interesting to watch the gondolier as he guides the little boat, turning corners as swiftly as a driver turns a street corner with horse and buggy, never once running into an object.

Notes of warning are called out continually as they glide along, and you are impressed with the thought of their carefulness. We hired a gondola for three hours, and did not get out of it during that time. The gondolier did not understand a word of English, so we could not talk to him; but we knew well enough what he meant when he stopped every once in a while. We shook our heads, No, no, and motioned for him to go on, when reluctantly he moved forward. You see Italians like strong drink, and he always pulled up in front of a saloon. When he could stand it no longer he did as he pleased and stopped for the drink, leaving us seated quietly in the boat.

Gondolas are all painted black, and most of them have cabins which serve to shield the passenger from sun or rain. They are very comfortable boats to ride in, and one does not get tired of skimming over the water. There is one canal larger than any of the rest, which is known as the Grand Canal. The water in it is deep enough to float large sized vessels, and many of them stop there to load and unload freight, and also to take on passengers for other ports. The water was perfectly calm, and our ride was interesting and enjoyable.

Venice is a very interesting city to visit, for there are many public buildings, such as the arsenal, which contains a museum of interesting objects, and Saint Mark's church. It alone would keep one occupied many days if he examined closely every object of interest in it; for it was constructed of the spoils of many buildings in almost every country in the far East. It has marble columns and panels dating back to the fourth century. It has been said that "St. Mark's body was brought to Venice secretly, from Alexandria, and placed in a vault in the chapel." We do not know how much truth there is in the guide's story; but, be that as it may, the church is a wonderful structure, and its panels, columns and mosaics are well worth examining.

Hundreds of pigeons have their nests in the cornice of St. Mark's, and no one dare drive them away. They ruin the beautiful molding, and one cannot help but wish it were different. The pigeons are quite tame, for they come down and sit upon the head, shoulders and hands of any one who will feed them. Some one bequeathed a certain sum of money for the feeding of the pigeons, and for years and years feed has been furnished them from the interest money. I am very fond of pets; so it pleased me greatly to see them come down by the hundreds for the food which was thrown them.

The streets were usually crowded with a set of lazy looking people, and we had a good chance to see them as we walked up one street and down another. There were many little shops where cooked victuals were on sale; in the windows could be seen crisp fried fish, and at the doors were large iron kettles filled with steaming hot boiled potatoes. Those articles were sold at reasonable prices, and I'm sure it was a convenience for the class of people who were too lazy to cook for themselves. The Italians are said to be a dirty set of people, and I am made to believe there is a good deal of truth in that saying.

By the time our party was ready to leave Venice we felt quite well acquainted with every street and canal, and to this day we look back with pleasure to the time when we visited the city of one hundred and fifty canals.

Our mind is now turned toward Athens, a city in Greece. Once again passage on a steamer was taken, for it proved to be the only way by which we were able to reach that place. There were seven of us now, and the personal conductor besides; yet not any of us had ever met before.

Trieste is an Austrian seaport town, and from there we sailed. The sea was as calm as a river, and sailing was delightful. Our first stopping place was at the Island of Corfu, where the anchor was cast and four hours spent in waiting for passengers. The whole company desired to go ashore, and after making proper arrangements with the boatmen were taken to land, where carriages were procured and a long drive in the country taken.

Oranges were plentiful in that country and little boys ran after the carriages just as fast as they could, wanting to sell their fruit. The party bought as many oranges as they desired, thinking the little fellows would discontinue the chase; but we were mistaken, for they followed on for miles, proving to be little nuisances.

Sea voyages are very tiresome, so the change was enjoyed by all, and the time spent on the steamer did not seem so long after the ride.

Piræus is the port of Athens, and is six miles from the city. Carriages had been ordered ahead, and we found them waiting at the landing. It took but a few minutes to settle ourselves in them, and we found the ride over the clean, broad, shaded road more agreeable than the rocking motion of a steamship. By this time you must surely know I am a lover of land, and prefer it to water. Reaching the city in an hour after, we were driven to a hotel on one of the principal streets.

The hotel was new, and the appearance pleasing. Many guests were there from different parts of the world, and every one seemed intent on seeing the sights of Athens. Very little time was spent in resting, for there was too much to be seen to spend time idly. Just in front of our hotel was the great public square, and at stated times the band played, bringing together crowds of people. Across the square from the hotel was the royal palace, built of beautiful white marble, and surrounding it were the palace gardens.

The language and customs of the people were different from those of other countries, and a guide was hired to take the entire party to places of interest as well as to talk for them. Each person was therefore privileged to ask questions, which he answered according to his best knowledge. The climate was mild, quite like that of Italy, and the exercise which walking gave kept us as warm as at home in the months of July and August.

Athens is not a city I should desire to have as a permanent place of residence, and we did not go there expecting to select a home; but we went to visit the city where years and years ago a great man introduced the Gospel. He was "of the stock of Israel, of the tribe of Benjamin, a Hebrew of the Hebrews." Who was that man? Ah, Paul! Yes, you think rightly; but he was not always a Christian; no; he persecuted them at one time, for you know he stood by and watched the stoning of Stephen, that faithful Christian man. If he had been a follower of Christ, such cruelty would not have been countenanced. Shortly after the stoning of Stephen the Lord called Paul, he was converted, and his boldness for the new cause was marvelous. Paul was an educated man, and able to talk to learned men wherever he went; and there was no end of Christian work for him to do.

The people in those times had kings to rule over them; so when Paul came around and told them of a person who was greater than their king, "one Jesus," it troubled them greatly. They were so enraged when Paul told about Jesus that it was feared the people would take his life. So he was sent away by night, and the place they took him to was Athens, the very city I've been writing about.

In Paul's time Athens was known all over the world as a city of great learning and one that paid great attention to the worship of the gods. In every direction could be seen temples, altars and other sacred buildings.

Mars' Hill is the place where the learned men took Paul, "saying, May we know what this new doctrine whereof thou speakest is? Then Paul stood in the midst of Mars' Hill and said, Ye men of Athens, I perceive that in all things ye are too superstitious." He had no fear of man, but gave them the truth without one bit of polishing. We stood on Mars' Hill, and called to mind the time when this great man was there preaching to the pleasure-loving, idol-worshiping Athenians. All around us were the ruins of the great temples of the time of Paul.

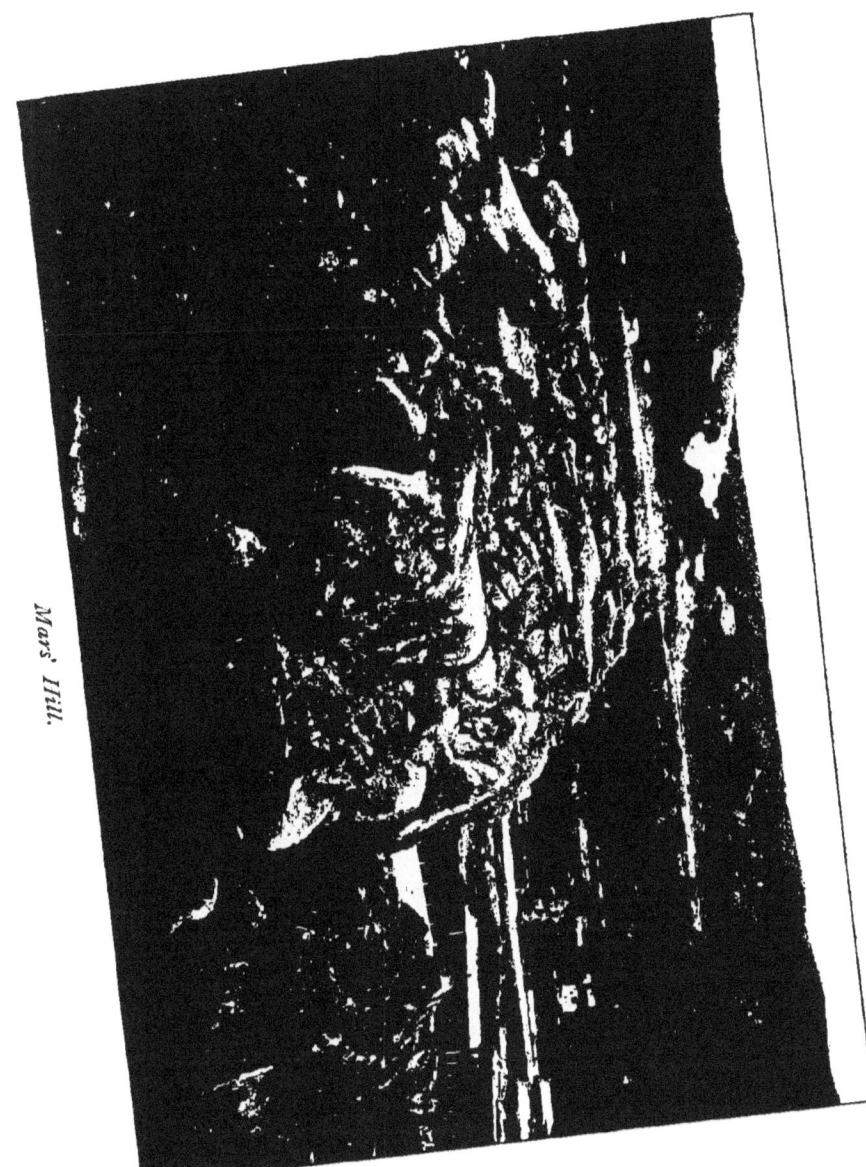

Mars' Hill.

Paul left Athens after this, and since then his great sermon has been read and reread; and these days many people turn to Christ through his wonderful preaching. Children, do you love the meek and lowly Jesus of whom Paul spoke? Think of it, my little readers, and may the Lord help you to be little workers for him.

All was not pleasure and joy while in Athens. Sickness comes to us whether at home or abroad, and many sad hours were spent at the bedside of the one who is very dear to me. The fever, which is so common in that country, fastened itself upon him, and the outlook seemed sad indeed to me. Many were the tears shed, and many were the prayers sent to the Father above, from the heart which seemed too heavy to perform its function; but the dear Father heard the prayers, and it was his will to raise the stricken one, so that the journey might be completed; and to-day we bless his name.

The time had come for us to leave Athens, and we were all taken back to Piræus, where we took ship for Smyrna. Three hundred miles were to be traveled on this trip, and then another rest. The wind blew quite hard at the start of the journey, and a rough voyage seemed to be in store for us; but we decided bad weather could be endured a couple of days, for soon rest would come. The wind had a splendid chance to blow, and after getting out into the open sea our little ship rolled and rolled, more than was agreeable to the poor creatures who were inclined to seasickness, and no doubt they wished for land; but the seasickness passed off after a while, and then the hollow-eyed people came forth from their staterooms to see whatever was to be seen along the way.

We passed an island and a city called Chios. Do you remember that Paul, on his journey, passed this very same island too? He did not stop there, because he was very anxious to reach Jerusalem by the day of Pentecost. Well, we did not stop either; our plans were to go right on, as we were on our way to Jerusalem too.

Sitting on deck was more agreeable to the passengers than remaining in the stateroom, so almost all of the time was spent on deck, even when the wind blew hard. One grew tired sitting all the time, so by way of change we walked back and forth. One time when we were sitting quietly a scream for help was heard; quickly every one of us rushed to the side of the ship, and there in the water below was a man. A sailor had been furling a sail—rolling it up—when, without a moment's warning, a strong gust of wind took him out to sea.

Life-buoys were fastened here and there along the railing of the ship, placed there to be used in case of necessity; that time had come, and quick as thought my husband cut the cords that bound one and immediately threw it far out in the water—toward the unfortunate man. By this time the excitement on board the ship was great. Other passengers cut loose life-buoys, and, strange to say, threw them out in quite a different direction from that in which the poor fellow was. The first buoy, however, was carried by a wave to the man. Almost breathless we stood watching him as he reached out and grasped the canvas-covered coil of cork. When his arm and head had been placed through it our breath came easier, for there was a possibility now of his being saved.

The steamer was stopped as soon as possible, and the anchor cast out to steady her, but by that time the man was far away, and he looked like a mere black speck in the distance. The captain stood by the railing of the ship, and in loud tones called to the unfortunate man to be brave and hold up, for soon help would come to him.

Three brave sailors manned one of the ship's boats, and when it was lowered faithfully and diligently rowed toward the dark speck in the distance. Everybody on that steamer watched the men, as nearer and nearer they drew to the object. What if he should drown? Just at that moment the unfortunate one was reached, then taken into the boat, and their faces soon after were turned shipward. Every dip of the oars brought them closer and closer to the ship, and oh how glad we were when at last their voices were heard near by. Steps were lowered, but the sea was so wild that every time the little boat came alongside of them a wave dashed it away. Finally they were successful, and soon after the dripping wet sailor stood before us.

The sailors who had gone to his rescue had great difficulty to get aboard the ship, and at times it seemed as though their little boat would surely be dashed to pieces. The sailor whose life had just been saved saw the perilous condition of his comrades and made a move to go to help them, but the captain seeing this in stern tones ordered him to go to his quarters. The man obeyed, but very reluctantly. The rest of the men came aboard shortly afterward, and once more quiet reigned.

I think I shall never forget with what sorrow we watched the poor fellow in the angry deep. His black hair and white face are still in my mind as we saw him floating along in the water, and his cry of distress still rings in my ears while I am writing this to you.

The language of the wet sailor was strange to us, and yet I knew he was unselfish. How did I know it? Because he had a desire to help his comrades when he in turn saw them in peril. A bruised body and dripping wet clothes were no hindrance to him; all was cast aside, and self was out of the question.

My little readers, can you not learn one good lesson from the conduct of the poor, half drowned sailor on the Mediterranean Sea? Yes, I believe you can. What is it? That of unselfishness. Help those who help you. Is that enough? No; no; go still farther; help those who are in distress, no matter whether they ever did a favor for you or not. Remember that deeds of kindness are never forgotten. Don't do acts of kindness for the reward; but because there is much love in your hearts for humanity. Cultivate a kindly disposition while young; and, believe me, you will be happier for it in after years.

Smyrna was reached at last, and just as the steamer reached the landing a large caravan of camels, about seventy in number, put in an appearance. A donkey with a man-upon his back led the caravan, and they were all joined together with a rope, the leader holding tight to one end of it. They moved along slowly in single file, looking quite awkward with the heavy burdens upon their backs. Camels are said to be patient and enduring. In case of a scarcity of water they are able to go without it for from eight to ten days. Horses and donkeys could not endure crossing the desert, but camels can, because their feet are cushion like, and therefore enlarge when placed upon the ground, making traveling easier for them when going through the sandy soil.

Smyrna is one of the cities which was spoken of in the Book of Revelation, and there one of the Seven Churches of Asia was located. A busy crowd of people were upon the streets, and in almost every direction dogs were seen in every attitude. One of the distressing things to me was the abundance of fleas which hopped upon us, biting as they went. We desired to keep away from dogs, but their home had been in Smyrna long enough to have the city well stocked with the little pests, and strangers were not long in finding it out, for, whether near by or far away from a dog, you were sure to be pestered.

The streets of Smyrna are narrow and dirty, with pools of disease-breeding water standing here and there upon them. The houses are not very large, and from the outside have an uninviting appearance. The dress of the people seemed odd, and indeed so did everything we looked at.

In walking over the city we saw many Mohammedan mosques, and near them was a tall, slender tower from which a priest called the hour of prayer. Now those towers are called minarets, and the priest is a muezzin. "Allah-el-Allah" is called in loud tones, and all the faithful ones bow down and pray; no matter whether they are buying a bill of goods or on their way to the mosque. We have seen them upon their knees on board of steamers, and they seemed not one bit afraid of attracting the attention of the tourists who stood looking on. Do you believe those people pray to be seen of men? We wondered about it, and since we have no right to judge we leave the matter with them.

Writing about Mohammedans brings to mind an incident which will no doubt interest you. On board the steamer was an ugly old man who had two wives and several children with him. They did not occupy staterooms, but took up their abode upon the deck, and were known as deck passengers. The women did not sit upon chairs, as did the rest of us, but flat upon the floor. As a shelter from the wind and the glances of the passengers an umbrella was used. We tried hard to peep under the covering to get a glimpse of the women's faces, but that privilege was never granted us, for the umbrella was sure to come between us. The old man walked back and forth for exercise, and the children ran to and fro before us; but the women never stirred from their first sitting place.

The wind blew very hard and the air was quite chilly even to those of us who were warmly clad. The children wore neither shoes nor stockings, and their clothing was of the thinnest kind of cloth. Their feet were pink with cold, and they had a season of crying as a result. The father was displeased, and raising a heavy stick which he carried let it come down upon the cold feet and ankles of the children. What a cruel act! And of course that kind of treatment brought forth cries louder than ever. In angry tones he scolded in a language we did not know, and quiet reigned when the sobbing little ones were taken under the umbrella with the women.

A guide accompanied us everywhere we went and talked for us, and as a party we kept him busy.

One beautiful, clear day we all went to Ephesus, another noted place of Bible times. The city once had a port and landing place for vessels, and its location at one time was such as to command great commerce; but these days the city is gone, and no port is to be seen; instead there are marshes which breed fever and disease, and every one who visits there fears to remain long lest the disease germ be taken into the system.

The people of Ephesus were given to the worship of idols, and not far from there was a temple called "the temple of Diana." Now Diana was a goddess, and the people thought she had come down from heaven; and they imagined she had the power to watch over all of their streams, and their wealth too. Well, in this temple were many beautiful things, for the wealthy people had beautiful gold and silver images made and placed there in honor of the great goddess, "whom all Asia and the world worshipeth." Each year there was a great display made of the images, for they were carried in a procession so that everybody could see them. The making of shrines and images became a great business, and many people were engaged in the work, and they grew rich from the proceeds. Paul was a missionary in the true sense. He never failed to tell the people wherever he went to believe on the Lord. You know from Athens he went to Corinth, and from there to the city I have been telling you about.

We read that he found disciples at this place and that he began asking them questions. He said to them, "Have ye received the Holy Ghost since ye believed?" And they told Paul that they had never heard of such a thing before. Immediately Paul told them they should believe on the Lord Jesus Christ. Quite willing were they to accept what Paul had told them, and after that were baptized. Then Paul laid his hands upon them, and about twelve disciples —quite a body of workers for the Lord—received the Holy Ghost, and after this they talked and prophesied.

The city was full of wickedness, so there was a splendid chance for Paul and the disciples to work; and very earnestly and faithfully they did work. When Paul began to preach the image-makers became alarmed; so much so that there was a great stir among them. A man by the name of Demetrius, who was a silversmith, became very angry. He called together the other workmen and sympathizers, and they, too, were angry. There was a wonderful time, "and the whole city was filled with confusion." They were not quieted until the town clerk talked to them. Don't you think there must have been a great time in Ephesus then? And don't you think Paul was a wonderful man to stay two years in a city like that, persuading the people to turn from their idols? For "all that dwelt in Asia heard the word of the Lord Jesus, both Jews and Greeks." Yes, he was a powerful preacher, and the Word of God grew and prevailed because of Paul's preaching.

The Lord does not countenance wickedness; so there came an end to the prosperity of Ephesus. Years and years ago the city and temple were destroyed; after which they were never rebuilt. Their ruins were covered up with mud and dirt for years, and so completely were they covered that no one knew exactly where their location was.

About twenty-four years ago a gentleman by the name of Wood hunted and dug until he found the ruins; then he worked faithfully until the temple of Diana was excavated. Now visitors have the pleasure of standing on the marble floors of the "temple of Diana of the Ephesians."

Instead of Ephesus, there stands a dirty little village called Ayasalouk, and here and there in the village can be seen marble columns and other pieces of fine marble taken from the once beautiful temple. The trip was an interesting one to us, because we knew that at one time Paul was in this very same country, and perhaps stood right where we stood.

Our stay at this place was not very long, for it was near train time, and we were compelled to go with the rest of our company. We tramped over the hills and among the ruins of Ephesus until we had gone eight miles. We were tired, and rest was welcome. A little before dark we were safe in Smyrna again, ready for a warm meal and a good rest.

Soon after this we left Smyrna for Jaffa. This time we had a distance of perhaps eight hundred miles to travel, and the voyage took five days. Many times we wished more of our traveling could have been upon land, and yet, when we think of it, many pleasant days were spent upon the sea, even though it was rough and stormy at times.

Our company consisted of Americans and English people, some from our own State,—Illinois,—some from New York. I must say that the most agreeable people of the company were Americans.

We took passage on the steamer Vesta, and Smyrna was left behind; we were started on our five days' journey to Jaffa. The voyage was pleasant and the scenery varied, for we passed many islands. Our boat stopped a short time at the Island of Cyprus, another one of Paul's missionary points and also the native place of Barnabas, who, having heard the bold speeches of Peter and John, sold his land "and brought the money, and laid it at the apostles' feet." Barnabas is frequently spoken of in the New Testament, for he was a good man and "full of the Holy Ghost and of faith;" and he, with Paul, made many missionary tours through this same Island of Cyprus.

About three hundred Greek and Armenian pilgrims wanted to be taken aboard at this place; but there were too many of them, the captain thought, so he took some and left the rest to wait for another ship. They made so much noise we felt almost sure there was some,disturbance brewing; but it proved to be only their earnest way of talking, for they seemed peaceable enough.

Each year hundreds of them make a pilgrimage to Jerusalem; they go there to enjoy the Easter ceremonies. Many of them walk from Jaffa to Jerusalem with pebbles in their shoes, or bare-foot. If some great sin has been committed, they take upon themselves some torture which may bring about suffering to the flesh.

The Vesta carried passengers who came from many parts of the world,—merchants, tourists and pilgrims,—some on their way to Jerusalem, others to Damascus, and still others to Egypt. There were ever so many Turks on board, and right outside of our stateroom were a number of Turkish women and children. There was a sofa in our stateroom by the window, and I often sat there listening to their strange language. I tried hard to see their faces, but that seemed out of the question, for the women were veiled, which is a custom among them. Occasionally the veil was thrown back, but just as soon as there was the least suspicion of any one looking at them it was hurriedly pulled down. The women who are seen with uncovered faces are considered bold.

The women and children were deck passengers, and during the trip stayed there close by my window. They had plenty of bedding which was very clean and nice looking. At night they slept upon it, and in the daytime used it to sit upon. The men kept baskets well filled with the finest of oranges, and no doubt there were plenty of good things besides for them to eat. The women wore large earrings in their ears, and the prevailing fashion among them was to stain the fingernails black; and thinking to add to their looks they put a streak of black under the lower eyelid.

One of the Turks had several women under his care, and among the number was a young girl whose father and mother were dead. She did not want to leave her home in Constantinople, but the man who had her in charge took her regardless of her wishes. This man was an uncle to the girl, and therefore had a right to do as he pleased; but it so happened that she never reached Damascus, the place aimed for.

There was great confusion among the Turkish women one night, and everybody on board the Vesta was aroused from slumber. Overhead there was an unusual amount of walking and talking, and above all could be heard the stern voice of the captain. We were very sure something had gone wrong, for the confusion lasted several hours and the captain seemed to have great trouble in quieting the people. After a while they settled down and we fell asleep. The next morning we learned that the young girl had disappeared during the night. All search seemed in vain, and after finding her clothing upon deck they concluded she had jumped overboard. Surely her Damascus trip was ended, and sad indeed must have been the heart of the poor, motherless girl who found a resting place in the Mediterranean Sea. That event brought sadness to our hearts, and

Woman with Veiled Face.

yet we had a strong desire to know more of the life of the poor Turkish maiden; but there was no need of dwelling longer on this subject, and therefore we cast it aside for more cheerful thoughts.

The weather was fine almost all of the trip, and much time was spent on deck watching the waves chase each other as we dashed along. Watching waves seemed like a trivial thing to do, but when passengers must depend upon themselves for amusement they are often intensely interested by the very smallest thing, especially when nothing is seen but sky and water for miles and miles and miles.

There are few secure harbors along the Mediterranean. Vessels always cast anchor out from shore from half a mile to a mile, and passengers as well as cargo must be taken ashore in small boats. If the sea should be boisterous the vessels are compelled to lie by until a calm; then discharge the cargo. That seemed to be our fate at Beyrut, for on reaching the port there was a stiff breeze which resembled a gale; and instead of stopping only a few hours we remained until the day following. The heavy sea twisted the Vesta and caused her to drag the anchor a little. We did not enjoy that part of it, for a restless, uneasy feeling in our stomach made us think of seasickness, which came very near following. Some passengers went ashore at Beyrut because it was the end of their journey, and others went for a change of scene. As we were not of the venturesome kind we decided to remain where we were until the next stopping place was reached, and that would be Jaffa.

Jaffa seemed very far away when we first thought of taking a journey through Palestine; but each day shortened the time until less than twenty-four hours remained, and then the next thing we knew the city was in view. The tourists commenced to talk about the dangerous landing and wish it were over with; and we of course were among the number.

Almost every one going to Jerusalem goes to the port of Jaffa. It is a very dangerous landing, because of its rocky coast. There are large, black rocks extending far out in the sea, and when the waves run high the little boats are dashed upon them, and all are lost. Sometimes ships are obliged to go on to the next port without landing a passenger or discharging the cargo.

There was so much noise and confusion at the landing, almost enough to scare a timid person. Boatmen crowded around the passengers and shouted at the top of their voices, each one trying to see how many passengers he could get, just like the cabmen at depots in our cities. I kept away from the noise as much as possible, and found a good hiding place in the stateroom, where they were not allowed to go. There I stayed until almost all the passengers had gone ashore.

There was a flight of steps on one side of the steamer, held in place by ropes, and quite a thick rope was used for a railing. The steps were used only by the passengers, and when needed no more by them were drawn up and fastened to the side of the ship. Those steps were somewhat shaky, for every time a person went down one step the whole flight took to shaking. Oh, how it made me tremble! for it seemed as though it were loose and would surely come down, and the passenger along with it. Sometimes the little boat was at the foot of the steps (for I have told you it was necessary to go ashore in small boats), and sometimes it was far away from them; so there was a quick movement needed if you were to be successful in getting in before a wave washed it away.

The boatmen are strong looking fellows, and the great sinews stand out on their arms so plainly that every one can be counted if you desire to do so. Their shirt sleeves were rolled up above the elbow, and no shoes were upon their feet. To see them is to impress one with their strength. One by one the gentlemen and ladies passed down the steps, each keeping his feelings to himself. Our turn came, so with weak and trembling knees we went down, keeping our eyes upon the boat which was tossing and pitching at a rapid rate at the foot of the steps. It seemed almost out of the question to step into it. Just as the attempt was to be made one of the Arab boatmen took me, and without much of an effort seated me in the little boat. The transfer was sudden, yet I shall always feel grateful for the kind act. Very cautiously the men rowed, passing between the rocks which were seen more plainly as we drew nearer and nearer the shore. No wonder all passengers dread the Jaffa landing, and no wonder many lives have been lost in landing when storms were raging.

Strong men are always glad when the ordeal of landing at Jaffa is over with. Is it any wonder then that timid women rejoice over the fact that there is only one Jaffa landing?

You can imagine we were rejoiced to be on solid ground again, and when the guide took us to the hotel we retired to our room; and there on bended knees we thanked our kind heavenly Father for his protecting care over us. Our hearts were full of thankfulness, and tears of gratitude filled our eyes. Though far, far from home, it was a pleasing thought to feel that the Lord was with us all the way.

CHAPTER VII.

Jaffa.—The Careless Camel.—Bible Characters who lived in Jaffa.—Jonah's Temptation.—On the Way to the Holy City.—An Arab and his Plow.—Ramleh.—Lydda in the Distance.—Leprous People Begging.—Leprous People of Bible Times.—Camp-fire in the Cave.—Jerusalem.—Our Room.—Solomon's Disobedience.—Tower of David.—The Stubborn Donkey.—Mohammedan Cemetery.—Mount of Olives.

JAFFA is built upon a hillside facing the sea, and the first glimpse of the flat-roofed stone houses, standing out as they did in the clear sunlight, is apt to cause one to pronounce the city beautiful; but wait until a walk through the narrow, dirty streets is taken, and such a thought as beautiful vanishes from the mind. A light shower of rain had fallen just before we arrived there; the filthy condition of the city was quite disagreeable, and it took away the desire to tarry long there.

While leisurely walking through one of the principal streets and feeling we were in no particular danger, except that of slipping down, we heard the guide call out, "Watch out!" I looked up, and to my surprise saw a camel loaded with orange boxes. The animal was very close to me, and a knock over the head seemed the next thing, for the boxes hung down, one on each side of him, and spread half way over the street. I thought quickly, and acted immediately, which means that I stooped down and the loaded orange boxes passed over my head. That act saved me from being walked over by the great, clumsy animal. That event did not discourage us, so we walked on and on.

We saw such odd looking little stores, dark and dirty. If a person desired to make a purchase it was done by standing out on the street and talking to the merchant who sat upon the floor of his store with legs crossed. What would you think if you saw shoemakers, blacksmiths and barbers all engaged in their special line of work, sitting upon the streets working with a will? That was no uncommon sight, but always an amusing one to us.

Oranges and lemons were plentiful in Jaffa, for there were several very large orchards near the city. We were there in the season to see the beautiful yellow fruit on the trees, and then to enjoy eating some of it. Florida oranges are fine, but I believe the Jaffa oranges are sweeter and more finely flavored.

But I must not spend too much time in telling you what we saw, for we are now in the Holy Land, and that brings to my mind the Bible characters who at one time walked those streets; for you know we are now writing about a very, very old city. Probably you can call to mind some of the people who lived there in Bible times, for I'm sure you have been studying about them in Sunday school.

You remember "Simon a tanner" who lived in Jaffa? Well, his house is pointed out to strangers, and is now being used as a mosque (house of worship). And you know Peter went on the housetop to pray. So in these days people go up on the top of that house and pray. Guides tell you a good many things in the course of a day, and one cannot always believe what they say. In all probability the location of this house is the same as the one which Simon lived in; but we are doubtful about the house.

I presume every girl and boy knows something about "Tabitha" or "Dorcas." She also lived in Jaffa; and you know we read she "was full of good works, and almsdeeds." One day she took sick and died, and her body was prepared for the tomb. Peter was not very many miles away, so he was sent for. Upon his arrival he was taken to the upper room where the lifeless body of Dorcas lay. Can you imagine the great sorrow of the people? "All the widows stood by him weeping and showing the coats and garments which Dorcas made while she was with them." And then what did Peter do? Why, he performed a great miracle, for he brought the good woman back to life again. That was a happy time, and there was real joy in that house. Everybody in Jaffa heard of Tabitha's sickness, death and restoration to life, "and many believed in the Lord."

Nineveh was a very wicked city, and the Lord was greatly concerned about it; so he called a man by the name of Jonah to go there and preach to the people. This man did not want to go, for no doubt he thought the work would be too hard; so he started to a place of his own choosing, and went to Jaffa, took ship there for Tarshish, paid the fare, went down in the ship and went to sleep. Do you believe he was altogether happy? We shall see by and by.

The Lord knew what Jonah was doing, and what was in his mind too, for you know nothing can be hid from the Lord, no matter how hard one tries. And this man found that out to his sorrow, for pretty soon "the Lord sent out a great wind into the sea, and there was a mighty tempest in the sea, so that the ship was like to be broken," and the sailors were dreadfully scared; but Jonah knew nothing about it, for he was fast asleep. As the storm grew in strength the seamen became more and more alarmed, and finally they called out, "Arise, call upon thy God." By this time the poor man was sure he was the cause of the stormy voyage. So Jonah said, "Take me up, and cast me forth into the sea." But they did not want to treat their passengers so unkindly; so they rowed and rowed, to see if they could possibly get to land with him and all be saved. But there was no use trying; the sea was too wild. Then they tried another plan; they called upon the Lord,—and very pitifully, too,—but that failed. "So they took up Jonah and cast him forth into the sea; and the sea ceased from her raging."

Now poor Jonah was in the water; but the Lord was not going to let him perish, so he prepared a great fish which swallowed him. Still the Lord was with him; and while in the great fish Jonah thought and "prayed unto the Lord his God." The Lord hears prayers and answers them if he thinks best; so this time poor Jonah's prayer was answered, and "the Lord spake unto the fish, and it vomited out Jonah upon the land." After that the Lord called him the second time, and this time he obeyed. He went and preached in Nineveh, and "the people of Nineveh believed God."

When Solomon decided to build a house for the Lord he sent word to "Hiram, king of Tyre," to send to him cunning workmen and also "cedar trees, fir trees, and algum trees out of Lebanon." The king was pleased to do as Solomon bade him, and as soon as it was possible sent a workman who was qualified to work in anything they saw proper to put him to. The timber was sent "in floats by sea to Joppa," and from there it was carried up to the city of Jerusalem, where the temple was to be built.

You will see by the instances which I have been giving that Jaffa must be an interesting place to visit, especially for those who love the Bible and its teachings. But our minds were turned toward the city of Jerusalem, and as soon as arrangements were made we started thitherward.

There were no signs of a railroad between the two cities then; so we had the privilege of choosing for ourselves whether we should take the trip in a carriage or on horseback. Our party preferred the carriage, thinking it to be the easier way of traveling over a rough, stony country.

Now the vehicle the guide called a carriage proved to be a very, very uncomfortable thing to ride in. At home it would have been called a covered spring wagon, and a very poor one at that. Sometimes we wondered whether it really had springs at all. But the guide called it a carriage, and we followed his example and called it a carriage too.

Jerusalem is between thirty and forty miles from Jaffa, and that meant an all day ride for us; and with the hope of reaching our destination that night we started. The morning was beautiful and the air fresh and bracing, so the change from sea to land travel was thoroughly enjoyed. Here and there along the road were cypress and sycamore trees, and occasionally an orange grove was passed. The sweet odor of the orange blossoms filled the air, and the perfume came to us while passing along. The beautiful yellow fruit could be seen hanging on the trees, and though it was too far away for us to touch, yet it was not too far to be admired.

There were many beautiful flowers growing along the highway, which seemed to be bowing a welcome to us. Our desire to pluck them was very great, but we rode on, finding it impossible to stop to gratify the desire, as the further we rode the more flowers we saw.

There were strange things along the way which interested us greatly. For instance, farmers were plowing their fields, and they had the oddest looking plows you ever saw. I'm not sure I shall be able to describe them; but you may imagine how they look when I tell you that a piece of wood, perhaps three feet long, is sharpened at one end, and at the other end a crosspiece is attached, which serves as handle. Now the sharpened end of the stick is the part which turns up the soil; and the furrows were not very deep, you may be sure. My husband had a desire to try plowing with an Arabic plow, so the first opportunity which was offered he put his hand to the plow and had a trial of it. The old Arab stood by, looking very much amused at the American's awkward attempt. The new plowman felt as though he would not like to make his living that way, so tarried but a little while.

Oxen, horses, donkeys and camels were used to draw the plows. Many times we saw a horse and an ox, or a horse and a donkey hitched together. But a great, tall, awkward camel seemed to be one of the strangest sights,— a great big camel, a little plow, and way behind all a poor little man. But you can imagine how it looked, and I'll leave you to smile over the thought of a camel being hitched to a little one-handled plow.

After riding ten miles we stopped for luncheon at a small village called Ramleh. A great tall square tower stands near the village, and almost every stranger climbs to the top of it; for from it may be seen the country round about. The steps show that many feet have trodden upon them, and the walls are badly cracked, showing to us that age was on its side. The village of Lydda, six miles distant, could be plainly seen from the top of the tower, and it seemed hardly possible that one's eyes could take in such a wide stretch of country at one glance.

You remember Lydda was the little village where Peter visited some of the saints. There he found a man by the name of Æneas who had been in bed eight years with palsy. "And Peter said unto him, Æneas, Jesus Christ maketh thee whole; arise, and make thy bed. And he arose immediately. And all that dwelt at Lydda and Saron saw him, and turned to the Lord."

This is also the little town to which two men were sent to find Peter after the death of Dorcas. You will see that from now on there will be very few miles passed over which will not have Bible history connected with them; and illustrations of Scripture may be gathered at almost every point.

Sitting by the roadside were a number of leprous people, both men and women. Now leprosy is a disease of the skin, and it eats away the flesh very much as does cancer; it is loathsome and incurable. According to law, every person afflicted with that disease must leave home and friends and live by himself, or with others who are suffering in the same manner.

When the people saw us every one of them arose and commenced begging. Arms with flesh eaten off and hands which were fingerless were held up to excite our sympathy. Oh, how horrible! for in some cases the flesh had been eaten away from the elbow to the wrist; the feet were without toes, and the faces in a distressing condition. The disease had gone to the lungs of some, for they coughed hard. The sight was touching, and our hearts ached for them. Small wooden pails were used to carry the money which was thrown them by benevolent people. This money was used in buying the necessaries of life for the whole company, for they lived together as one family among the ruins of old houses outside of the city, as they are not allowed to come inside of any city.

There are many leprous persons spoken of in the Bible, and I shall mention a few of them. First, then, was Miriam, the sister of Aaron and Moses. One day she and Aaron spoke against Moses, which fact displeased the

Lord; and as a punishment to Miriam she "became leprous, white as snow." The brothers felt dreadfully bad to know of their sister's affliction. "And Moses cried unto the Lord saying, Heal her now, O God, I beseech thee." After having seen people with leprosy once you may not expect soon to be rid of the sickening sight, for it will surely remain in your mind. And now, while writing this to you, the sight of those poor creatures comes to me, and I do not wonder that Moses pleaded for the healing of Miriam.

Naaman, you remember, was a great man; but he had the leprosy. Now this man's wife had a little captive maiden working for her, who seemed greatly interested in the leprous man; so one time the maiden said to her mistress, "Would God my lord were with the prophet that is in Samaria; for he would recover him of the leprosy." Some one told the great man what the little maiden had said; so the king of Syria sent a letter to the king of Israel, and with it sent many pieces of silver and ever so many pieces of gold, and also several changes of raiment.

When the king of Israel received and read the letter, he could not understand why it had been sent to him, and concluded that the king of Syria wanted to quarrel with him. He was therefore very much displeased.

Elisha, the man of God, heard of the letter and knew what it meant; so he sent to the king, saying, "Wherefore hast thou rent thy clothes? Let him come to me, and he shall know that there is a prophet in Israel. So Naaman came with his horses and chariots and stood at the door of the house of Elisha." Well, Elisha told Naaman what he should do to be made whole; but the great man grew very angry and went away in a rage. Naaman's servant said, "My father, if the prophet had bid thee do some great thing, wouldst thou not have done it? How much rather then, when he saith to thee, Wash and be clean?"

After this Naaman did as Elisha had directed, and he was made clean of the dreadful, humiliating disease. The little captive maiden was far from home and friends, and no doubt was sad many times because she could not see her mother and father; yet, in her loneliness, she did not forget to let her light shine for good; she was thoughtful of those around her, and because of her thoughtfulness Naaman was brought to visit the prophet, and then to know of the God who rules over all.

Gehazi was the servant of Elisha. He did wrong by asking Naaman to give something for his healing, which he knew was not in accordance with the desire of Elisha's heart. Then, when questioned about the matter, he told an untruth, and the doom pronounced upon Gehazi was this: "The leprosy therefore of Namann shall cleave unto thee, and unto thy seed for ever. And he went out from his presence a leper as white as snow." The Lord does not countenance wickedness in any shape or form, and punishment is in store for all who do wickedly.

Children, are you ever tempted to be untruthful? Oh, be careful! Remember the Lord knows all; he hears you and sees everything you do. When you do wickedly it grieves him, and is it right for you to grieve the best friend you have? No, no.

It was late in the afternoon when we left Ramleh, so we rode only a few hours before daylight disappeared. Riding was not very pleasant after dark, for the road over the mountains was rough and stony.

After traveling several miles, a small village was reached, where we rested a short time. There is an inn or lodging place at this point, and many persons stop there all night. It was a dirty looking place, for the lower part of the house was used as a stable for horses. Some travelers prefer camping out and I'm pretty sure I would rather camp out than sleep in such a place as that; but our intentions were to sleep in Jerusalem that night, and that being the case we rested but a short time.

Our guide was unusually slow in having the horses brought up, so a few of us walked on up the mountain. We had walked but a short distance when dark clouds were seen overhead; by and by rain came down, and a thorough drenching seemed in store for us. Shelter was found, however, under the wide-spreading branches of an olive tree, and there we stood until, to our sorrow, it began to leak, and the water commenced dropping upon us-uncomfortably fast. But by this time a rumbling noise was heard in the distance, and our carriage came in sight. In a very little while after we were seated in it, about as uncomfortably as could be imagined. Some of the party had walked farther on, so were not taken in at this point. The darkness seemed more dense now and the road dreadfully bad. Away in the distance a bright light was seen, and men could be seen moving about quite lively before their campfire.

Highway robbers came into our mind, but there was not time to harbor such thoughts long, for on getting a little closer to them we found two of our traveling companions who had gone into a cave for shelter from the rain. For amusement and warmth they had, Arab like, built a fire. The men were full of fun, and their antics were quite grotesque. You can scarcely imagine how funny they did look, dancing before the blazing fire. Of course all laughed, for we could not help ourselves. Their shelter from the rain was a good one, and there was no danger of its leaking either. All were settled in the carriage at last, so we drove on.

As we neared the top of the mountain another campfire was seen, but this time it was that of a Greek caravan which had stopped for the night. There were ever so many men, camels and donkeys, and the bright fire looked quite cheerful, for we were pretty well chilled; but we did not stop, for if Jerusalem was to be reached that night it was necessary for us to keep moving.

The roads continued bad, very bad. Many places there were great, deep gullies washed out; the wagon wheels dropped into them with a thud, and at times it seemed as though the wagon would surely go over. Some of the party concluded to try walking, that they might keep warm—a good thing for them to do. I'm very sure the footmen had a more pleasant time than we who were riding. At times we were almost thrown from our seats by the jolting, and I clung to the back of the seat in front of me. I did not hesitate to pronounce it the worst ride which I had ever taken. Oh, how we did wish for starlight or, better still, moonlight; but neither stars nor moon could be seen. The guide and drivers felt the need of refreshments very often, and when another coffeehouse was reached they stopped while we all waited, sitting in the wagon, trying to be patient. After all, the men did us a favor by stopping, for just as we were ready to start a break in the clouds was seen, and to our delight the beautiful moon came forth and lighted our way. It was just what we had been wishing for, and from there on the gullies could be seen plainly, and groping in darkness was at an end.

Somewhere on that road our Savior joined two disciples who were on their way to Emmaus, "which was from Jerusalem about three score furlongs."

Jerusalem is surrounded by mountains; so the last few miles of our ride was up hill. The pleasure of seeing the city by moonlight was granted us, and it seemed to me the moon never did shine more brightly than on that night.

The guide said, "We are now not far from Jerusalem"; and on looking in the direction in which he pointed the dim outlines of the high walls were seen. "Is it really the walls of Jerusalem?" we asked, and no answer was needed, for shortly after the carriage stopped and all stood at the Jaffa Gate, one of the entrances to the city. The guide took us to the hotel; and a tired company of tourists we were. The ride over the mountain had chilled us to the bone, but there was no fire to greet us. The meal which had been prepared was likewise cold, and when a cup of tea was passed us it too was disappointingly cold and seemed to have been far from fire an hour or more. What a reception! Will you be surprised to know that thoughts of home and loved ones came thick and fast?

It was midnight, and when the servant took us to our room, imagine our feelings on beholding the flooring to be of stone and iron bars across the one small window. A shudder passed over us, and we thought of a prison cell. Two beds were in the room. Upon examination we found there were two linen sheets to sleep between and a very poor, thin comfort for covering. The outlook for getting warm was not very bright, and I still have recollections of shivering until almost morning.

The window I made mention of seemed entirely out of place so close to the ceiling, and it was always a wonder to me why the builders placed it so high. And then, why the iron bars? When alone in my room one day the thought struck me this way, "I'll see why the window is so high." And forthwith the wash-stand was moved under it, and in a short time after I stood upon it. Even then I came near being too low; but by standing on my tiptoes and then stretching my neck until it seemed the leaders were strained I succeeded in looking out. I did not see people passing, but instead found the window looked down upon a great pool. It was well filled with water which had run into it during the rainy season. The pool, it is thought, had been built by Hezekiah who was king of Jerusalem many, many years ago. Since the pool was all that could be seen

One of Solomon's Pools.

from the window and I was not anxious to remain longer in such a strained position, I decided to go where a better view could be had of it. My curiosity had been gratified, and I never looked out of that window again. Soon after this the guide came, and we all started out to see the city.

Solomon's pools are only a few hours' ride from Jerusalem and may be seen on your way to the city of Bethlehem. They are three in number, and all of them are of great size. We learn there is one which is considered finer than the rest, and its dimensions are one hundred and ninety-four yards long, forty-nine yards wide at the top, and sixty-nine yards below, and is at places forty-eight feet deep, and hewn in the rock.

You have a very good picture of one of the pools in the engraving, and when looking at it just think that ancient Jerusalem was partly supplied with water which had been stored away in it, and that probably the gardens, the orchards, and the trees of all kinds of fruits, which Solomon speaks of having planted, were watered by them, for we read, "I made me pools of water, to water therewith the wood that bringeth forth trees."

There was so much to be seen in and around Jerusalem. We scarcely knew what place to visit first, but the guide settled the matter for us by taking the party to a Mohammedan church, the Mosque of Omar, as it is called.

I wonder how many of you know anything about Solomon. Well, I'll tell you. Solomon was the son of David, and a very wise man. "And Solomon's wisdom excelled the wisdom of all the children of the east country, and all the wisdom of Egypt, and he spake three thousand proverbs: and his songs were a thousand and five." He was such a wise man that the people and the kings went to hear him.

The Lord had said to David one time, "Thy son whom I will set upon thy throne in thy room, he shall build a house unto my name." Well, Solomon decided to build the house, and it proved to be a wonderfully fine building. Its foundation was of costly stone, and there was a great deal of brass used; and when the inside of the building was finished it was overlaid with pure gold. After the temple was finished it was dedicated to the Lord, and Solomon prayed a long, long prayer.

Well, the Lord heard the prayer of Solomon, and said, "If thou wilt walk before me, as David thy father walked, in integrity of heart, and in uprightness, to do according to all that I have commanded thee, and wilt keep my statutes and my judgments: then I will establish the throne of thy kingdom upon Israel forever. But if ye shall at all turn from following me, ye or your children, and will not keep my commandments and my statutes which I have set before you, but go and serve other gods, and worship them; then will I cut off Israel out of the land which I have given them: and this house, which I have hallowed for my name, will I cast out of my sight; and Israel shall be a proverb and a byword among all people."

Years rolled on, Solomon served the Lord faithfully; but by and by he grew weak, sinned against the Lord, and worshiped gods made by hand. He did just what the Lord forbade him to do, and the result was the utter destruction of the temple. Not one stone was left upon another; and the Mohammedan church — the Mosque of Omar — now stands on the site where once stood Solomon's Temple.

The Lord was kind to Solomon after all, for the kingdom was not taken from him, but was taken from the hand of his son. Remember that punishment is always sure to follow evil-doing.

The Mohammedans do not allow any one to go into their mosques with shoes on, so each one of the party had to remove his shoes and put on a pair of slippers. The interior of a Mohammedan mosque is considered sacred, almost too much so for the feet of Christians to press. A few years ago Christians could not gain an entrance at all, but of late they are allowed the privilege. A guide always accompanies them, however, and takes pleasure in pointing out the interesting objects which the dark, gloomy mosque contains.

There is an old tower near the Jaffa Gate called the "Tower of David," and it is supposed to be the only building standing which the Lord may have gazed upon.

The streets of Jerusalem are so narrow that carriages and wagons cannot be used. Men, camels and donkeys carry all the burdens; and it is just as necessary for pedestrians to be on their guard in that city as it was in the city of Jaffa, for camels and donkeys would just as lief walk over you, as they never turn out of the road.

Here is an amusing incident which I saw while standing upon the veranda of our hotel. There was a market place just opposite the hotel, and I stood watching the people sell their cauliflower, onions and other vegetables. Purchasers were not very numerous that morning, and the sales were rather dull. One old woman was sitting near her stand of vegetables almost asleep. Far behind her was a man trying very hard to get his donkey to turn in a direction different from the one in which it persisted in going. Pounding over the head with a club seemed to make no impression upon the feelings of the animal, and the stubborn donkey budged not an inch. By and by there was a change of treatment; the little animal was taken up bodily and turned around. Immediately he started off, not caring where, and ran right over the old woman, upsetting her and scattering the vegetables all around. Oh, how surprised she looked to find herself tumbled in a heap; and when she beheld the donkey a look of, Oh, well, one need expect nothing else from you, came into her face; then quietly the scattered vegetables were picked up. The vegetables were not injured, and the only thing distressing about the whole affair was that the market woman lost her nap, for afterwards she seemed quite wide awake.

In the city of Jerusalem? Yes, and how strange! It would be impossible to try to describe our feelings, for we knew that somewhere in that vicinity holy men of old had lived and walked and preached. We were aware of the fact that the city had been destroyed many times since Christ's time, and that the streets which he was wont to walk upon were covered up with many feet of earth. Yet, notwithstanding that fact, we felt wonderfully blessed in being allowed the privilege of even being in the land where Christ and his disciples loved to dwell. Solomon reigned over Jerusalem forty years. God told Abraham to offer his only son for a burnt offering on Moriah, and there the Temple of Solomon was built. I could spend many hours writing about the patriarchs of old, but must hasten on and tell you just a little more about the city. It is surrounded by a high wall pierced with many gates. Every one who goes into or out of the city must pass through one of these gates. A few years ago every one of them was closed after sundown, but no attention is paid to locking them now, and you are allowed to go in and out any hour of the night.

Many of the stones in one portion of the wall are very, very old, and the Jews think they were used at one time in the foundation of their ancient temple, and that is as near as it is possible for them to get to the Holy of holies; so every Friday—and other days too—they gather together and weep and wail over the downfall of their beloved Zion. That place is always known as the "Jews' Wailing Place."

There is a Mohammedan cemetery outside of the city wall; the graves are about two feet high and are covered with a white coat of plaster. There are no tombstones and no names to tell the passer-by whose remains lie beneath the sod. Possibly the relatives know by the location where their dead are buried, but I'm pretty sure no one else could tell. One afternoon we had walked a long distance, and on our return to the hotel passed through the cemetery I've just told you about. We were very tired, so leaned against a tomb to rest a few minutes. Several Moslem men passed us, muttering to themselves, and looking quite savage. We asked, "What ails them?" and the reply was, "They don't want their graves desecrated by Christian dogs." That was the first time we had been likened to a dog; and, fearing the compliment might be repeated, we arose immediately and walked away. The Mohammedans' love for a Christian is not great, and it was a little uncertain how many insults they might be tempted to offer if we tarried longer.

Go with me now, my little readers, to the Garden of Gethsemane, to which place it is said Jesus often went with his disciples. We found it at the foot of the Mount of Olives, surrounded by a low stone wall. A monk acted as guide and never left our side until the gate was closed against us on our departure. The garden is well kept. Flowers here and there with nice graveled walks make the place rather inviting to visitors who usually go there soon after reaching the city. There are several old olive trees in the garden, and it is thought they are the same trees under which the blessed Master wept and prayed. When we looked at them this saying of his came to our mind, "My soul is exceeding sorrowful, even unto death; tarry ye here, and watch with me." And he went a little farther, and fell on his face, and prayed. Oh, what a sorrowful prayer, for he said, "O my Father, if it be possible, let this cup pass from me: nevertheless not as I will, but as thou wilt." Truly he was acquainted with grief. It is useless to attempt to tell you all of the instances connected with the scene, so we leave the garden and ascend the Mount of Olives.

Somewhere on the Mount of Olives, after his resurrection, Jesus was carried up to heaven. When David fled from Jerusalem he wept as he went up this same mount. Ezekiel tells us that "the glory of the Lord went up from the midst of the city, and stood upon the mountain which is on the east side of the city." Thus you see both the Old and the New Testament refers to Olivet; and could the stones be made to speak many a tale of sadness would be told by them.

CHAPTER VIII.

Bethany.—Bethlehem.—Rachel's Tomb.—The Shepherd Boy.—Ruth and Naomi.—Garden of Gethsemane.—Departure from Jerusalem.—Yosef.—Jericho Road.—Ain-es-Sultan.—Morning Call.—Donkey Boy. —Dead Sea.—Along the Banks of the Jordan.—John the Baptist. —Bad Roads.

BETHANY is perhaps two miles from Jerusalem. At one time it was the home of Mary, Martha and Lazarus, a family whom Jesus dearly loved to visit when tired of the noise and confusion of the city. Sickness and death came to that family, and the brother was taken from them and placed in the tomb. When Jesus heard of their distress he said to his disciples, "I go that I may awake him out of sleep." And when the home was reached and the burial place of Lazarus pointed out "Jesus wept;" and at his command the stone was taken from the cave and Lazarus was brought to life, even though he had been in the grave four days. The unbelieving crowd saw Jesus had power to make alive, and the result was many "believed on him."

There was not much to be seen in the little village,—a church, a few houses, and very many beggars,—and as the day was well spent we all decided not to tarry very long, but to return to the hotel in the city of Jerusalem and rest, for every one of us was tired. Our tramps were always long ones, and at the close of a day rest was sweet.

I presume there are but few of you who have not heard of "Bethlehem of Judea." It is spoken of as "Ephrath," and is known to be the birthplace of David and Christ

We left Jerusalem by the Jaffa Gate, a party of eighteen, and every one mounted upon the back of a horse. Our company consisted of two Australians, seven Englishmen, two Germans, one Scotchman, and six Americans. Eight of the number were women. Not one of the party was under the age of thirty-five years. You will see that none of us were children.

My experience in horseback riding was quite limited, therefore I did poorly. The rest were good riders because they had experience. We got along pretty well, and the practice of that day prepared us all for the many days of hard riding which followed. The desire to be upon my feet, rather than upon the back of a horse, was never quite overcome.

Our horses seldom got out of a walk, because of the poor condition of the roads. Fast riding in Palestine is very seldom engaged in, and as a rule horses have their own way, regulating their gait to suit themselves. A number of people were on the road, walking and riding donkeys. The animals were so small that when the riders' feet hung down they touched the ground, which sight amused us greatly. Our English sidesaddles were quite a novelty to them, and they scarcely raised their eyes higher than where the saddles were located. In their minds the Arabs were probably comparing the neatness of our saddles to the clumsy looking things used by them.

Bethlehem is about six miles from Jerusalem, and those six miles seemed very long ones to us, for the road was hard to travel. The country was extremely stony, and we wondered how grain could find soil in which to sprout. Fields were passed from which enough stones had been picked to make a fence which was, perhaps, one mile in length and wide enough for several horsemen to ride abreast upon it.

Before reaching Bethlehem a shower of rain came up and the guide took us into the tomb of Rachel for shelter. The tomb was well filled with Arab men and women who had gone there before us, and when we all appeared before them they scattered at a lively rate. Getting close to a party of Christians would no doubt have made them very uncomfortable, so they preferred to vacate.

Many, many years ago Jacob and Rachel were making a journey to Bethlehem, and when but a short distance from the city "Rachel died, and was buried in the way to Ephrath, which is Bethlehem. And Jacob set a pillar upon her grave: that is the pillar of Rachel's grave unto this day."

Long, long ago the pillar which had been set up by Jacob disappeared; but in its place stands a small white building with a dome. It is by the roadside, and everybody looks upon it as marking the last resting place of Jacob's beloved wife. It is known all around as "Rachel's Tomb,"

Rachel's Tomb by the Roadside.

and it was into this tomb that we were taken to escape the falling rain.

During the reign of king Saul there was a man who was known as Jesse the Bethlehemite, and he had a large family of very fine looking boys. The Lord desired to make a new king to reign in the place of Saul, and one of Jesse's sons was to be the fortunate one. Samuel—and you know who he was?—was appointed by the Lord to go and anoint the new king. But poor Samuel was dreadfully afraid of king Saul, and said, "How can I go? If Saul hear it, he will kill me." But the Lord doeth all things well in every instance, and in that matter he was not slack. "And Samuel did that which the Lord spake, and came to Bethlehem."

One by one the sons of Jesse were looked upon, but the Lord was not satisfied with any excepting the very youngest, and he was a shepherd boy "ruddy, and withal of a beautiful countenance, and goodly to look upon." Well, Samuel anointed him king to reign in the place of Saul, and David was the boy's name. I have often wondered whether he ever thought such a high position would be given him. When the Lord desires workmen these days he is just as liable to call them from the humble walks of life as he did David, and remember he is watching you, and knows whether you will be fit for his work; and no matter whether you are a farmer's boy or a homeless bootblack, when the Lord is ready he will call you.

This is, in a few words, the story of David the shepherd boy who was made king in the place of Saul. Well, David came to be a great man and everybody looked on him as such. He fought many battles, and in the "war between the house of Saul and the house of David he grew stronger and stronger."

David had several sons and among the number was one whose name was Absalom, and there was no one who received more praise for his beauty than this third son of David, for we read that "from the sole of his foot even to the crown of his head there was no blemish in him." Absalom had a fine head of hair and each year it was cut and weighed, and the weight of it was astonishingly great. Now with all of his good looks—like many another young man—Absalom was wicked, for he conspired against David and stole the hearts of the people. The poor father was not aware of the deceitfulness of his son until "there came a message to David, saying, The hearts of the men of Israel are after Absalom," and then to escape the violence of the wicked son he "went forth, and all his household after him, and tarried in a place that was far off." Don't you believe that was a sorrowful sight when "David went up by the ascent of mount Olivet, and wept as he went up"? Just think of him hurriedly walking over the stones in his bare feet, and then think "all the people that was with him covered every man his head, and they went up, weeping as they went up." Just think of the distress and heartache brought about by the action of one wayward boy. Even though the father is made to suffer yet he loves the son, and when David sent forth men to battle he gave this command, "Deal gently for my sake with the young man, even with Absalom." The sword did not cut him asunder, but we read that "Absalom rode upon a mule, and the mule went under a bough of a great oak, and he was taken up between the heaven and the earth: and the mule that was under him went away. And a certain man saw it, and told Joab, and said, Behold, I saw Absalom hanging in an oak," and that was the fate of a boy who loved self more than any one else. But how do you imagine David felt when tidings of the son's death were brought him? When the runner who brought the news was near enough to hear David's voice, he called out, "Is the young man Absalom safe?" And again we read that he wept; "and as he went, thus he said, O my son Absalom! my son, my son Absalom! would God I had died for thee, O Absalom, my son, my son!" When it was told how the king was weeping "the victory that day was turned into mourning unto all the people."

Young people are prone to be ambitious, and that is all right; but, dear young people, don't let your ambitious desires cause you to disobey father and mother and bring sadness and sorrow upon those who love you. Think of sorrowing David, and then think of the beautiful son's final end, and may you learn from it what is becoming a child.

The tomb of Absalom is before you. We do not know by whom it was built, but it is thought that it marks the site of the pillar which "Absalom in his lifetime had taken and reared up for himself, which is in the king's dale," and this tomb is in the valley east of Jerusalem.

The touching story of Ruth and Naomi comes to my mind while I write, and my heart goes out in sympathy toward those lonely widows who perhaps walked along the very road which we traveled over. The fields of Boaz were no doubt quite near to Bethlehem, and I think of his kindness to Ruth when he said, "Go not to glean in another field, neither go from hence, but abide here fast by my maidens;" and then later on he said, "Let her glean even among the sheaves, and reproach her not." Truly a good man was Boaz, and a deserving woman was Ruth.

There lived in Nazareth a man by the name of Joseph, and a woman whose name was Mary. A law had been passed that all the world should be taxed, so "all went to be taxed, every one in his own city." Mary and Joseph traveled a long, long distance, and upon their arrival in the city found, to their sorrow, that there was no room for them in the inn. They were tired, weary and almost sick, and had no place to rest. Oh, what a trying time for them. While waiting to be taxed a child was born, a little baby boy; and his mother "wrapped him in swaddling clothes, and laid him in a manger; because there was no room for them in the inn." That seemed like a poor place for the tender infant, but the angels kept good watch over him. The name of the child was Jesus, and his birthplace was Bethlehem; and he proved to be the Savior of the world, for when he reached manhood he suffered and died that you and I might live. "The Church of the Nativity" is said to cover the spot where Jesus was born; but we shall

Absalom's Tomb.

never know for certain how much truth there is in the saying.

At the close of the day spent in Bethlehem the guide informed us we had ridden almost twenty miles, and with astonishment we said, "No wonder we were tired and weary." Arrangements had been made for us to start the following day on a long journey, which would take twenty-one days to complete. Our home was to be in tents, and every mile of the road was to be traveled over on horseback. Horses and mules were to carry baggage, beds and bedding, dishes, cook stove and food. Trunks were left behind, because much baggage was not allowed.

From now on we shall call our guide "the dragoman," which means interpreter. Mr. Heilpin

A Dragoman.

spoke seven or eight languages with ease. He was a tall, well-built man with commanding appearance. We were impressed with the thought that he was quite able to take care of a large party of dependent tourists.

We were to have left Jerusalem at an early hour in the morning, but a heavy rain storm hindered us from starting at the appointed time. After the rain slackened a little all started to the place where the horses stood saddled and bridled. Just as we were about to mount, the rain came down wonderfully fast, and there was somewhat of a desire to turn back and take shelter in the hotel. Mr. Heilpin, the dragoman, would not hear to it, and when he gave the order to go, we murmured not, but went. The outlook was not very pleasant: to turn back was out of the question, and a ride of twenty miles was to be made before reaching our camping place in the evening. We moved on, bearing very sad looking faces and trying hard to make the best of it.

Our journey took us by the Garden of Gethsemane and over the Mount of Olives, the same road over which Christ rode on the back of a colt, on his way to Jerusalem. We never expected to see the Holy City again, and at this point we turned, looking back, and in our hearts we said, Farewell, City of David, farewell.

The rain had ceased by that time, and the sun came forth bright and hot; only for a little while, however, for in a very short time the rain came down as fast as ever. My rain cloak seemed to protect me but poorly, for by this time a good deal of water had gone through my clothing and it was pretty well soaked.

Noontime came. We stopped in a dirty, dreary looking cave to eat our luncheon. The servant who attended to our wants spread a cloth upon the ground, and upon the cloth was placed the food which had been prepared in Jerusalem. All of the party but myself sat around the cloth. I stood up and ate what little was needed. As soon as possible I went out and stood in the sun, which was again shining. Between the sun and wind I was made more comfortable, and by the time we were ready to start my clothing was quite dry. After luncheon we mounted our horses and were again on our way to Jericho.

Somewhere on that road perhaps the good Samaritan came across the poor man who had fallen among thieves, who had been stripped of his clothing, wounded and left half dead. The road is considered unsafe yet, for thieves still act unkindly toward those who travel over it.

Yosef was the name of the servant who helped with luncheon. He was quite thoughtful of those in the party who called upon him, and always willing to do their bidding. Much of the time he was found at my side, for I seemed to be the one who needed him. He was a great fellow to talk, and he chattered away leaving me to guess at what he was saying. His English was limited, and I knew no Arabic at all, so it kept both busy trying to think out what the other had said.

One time Yosef looked up in my face and called very cheerily in Arabic, "Ain-es-Sultan, Ain-es-Sultan," and while calling pointed with his finger off in the distance. Repeatedly I said, "I don't understand you, Yosef." And again the same "Ain-es-Sultan" was called out, and he motioned with his head, as much as to say, Yes, there it is, away over there. But what was it? That was the question. "What does Yosef want to tell us?" we asked the dragoman. "He is trying to tell you we shall soon be at the Prophet's Fountain,"—the very one which Elisha threw salt into. It is said that all the water around there is poor; but we know the water in the Prophet's Fountain is splendid.

Our camping place was on a high knoll near the flowing fountain, and when the camping place was reached a beautiful sight met our gaze. Before us were eleven white tents, and floating above one of them was the American flag,—the Stars and Stripes. As my eyes fell upon it I called out to the American portion of the party, "Look at the old flag; how I wish it might fly above our tent."

It took but a short time to dismount, but a much longer time to stand straight after being upon our feet. Men know nothing of the torture women must endure sitting sidewise on a saddle. But we got all right after a while. When a tent was assigned us we forthwith went to it; and there, sure enough, the old flag was flying above it. The sight of it made me homesick. Yes, I thought of America, so far away, and my eyes filled brimful of tears. There was no time for tears, so I brushed them away and in a very short time after we were all called to dinner.

After dinner was over the dragoman informed us that he had a chest which he slept upon every night, and that our watches, money and valuables should be handed to him for safe keeping. Furthermore he said: "In each tent will be found a long piece of rope; use it in tying your loose baggage to your bedstead. Your clothing, boots and shoes you will put in as safe a place as possible." When he finished his remarks we seemed spellbound; but we were at Jericho, and we knew the reputation of the country was not any better than it used to be. The servants kept watch all night, and yet, notwithstanding that, the natives could have crawled into the tents and taken everything within their reach if any of them had chanced to be around.

There were nine sleeping tents, and each person had an iron bedstead with mattress, two linen sheets, one blanket, a white spread and one pillow with a case upon it; and every one of the tents was numbered. The number of ours was nine. All of the party seemed to have enjoyed the good, warm meal, and a little time was spent in talking of what had been seen during the day. But bedtime came and each one retired to his tent. After tying the baggage to our bedsteads, placing boots, shoes and clothing under our head and feet, we crawled into the little beds. Sleep overcame us, and in a little while we were in dreamland. My sleep was broken, for every movement outside of the tent caused my eyes to open wide, and much time was wasted in looking for the thieving Arab who never put in an appearance.

Hyenas and jackals are numerous in that country, and during the nights they bark long and loud. Sometimes they seemed not very far from the camp. Very likely they would have ventured into camp; but a bright fire was kept burning, and seated around it were the watching servants.

Early the next morning all hands were aroused by the rattling of tin pans which were in the hands of the servants. The banging noise was distressing to listen to, and we wished the pans were far enough away. Some were slow to rise, even with such deafening noise. But they soon learned that it was useless to even think of taking a second nap after the first banging of pans. Every morning from that on the deafening music was heard. Breakfast was always ready for us, and no time was wasted in waiting.

Our meals were usually very good. There was tea, coffee, bread, butter, eggs and omelette,—composed of eggs, milk and salt. Condensed milk was used for coffee; the butter was canned too; it was never fresh, but always very soft. A little of it went a great ways. Indeed, many times it was left untouched by us. We did not tarry very long after breakfast on the camp ground, for our horses were saddled and the dragoman waiting to take the party to the Dead Sea and the Jordan.

The modern village of Jericho was passed through, and not a house was to be seen; nothing but Bedouin Arab tents. You know Jesus passed through Jericho on his way to Jerusalem. There Zaccheus lived, and you remember he was small of stature. He wanted to see Jesus when he passed by, but the crowd was so great that there was no chance for him; so he ran ahead of the crowd and climbed up a tree, and there he could see all who passed.

Our riding was usually done single file, for all through that country the roads are bad. The sun was extremely hot, and a nice shade would have been agreeable to all; but we could not choose the path, so we journeyed on and on.

The people in that part of the country are not very thrifty,—more inclined to be lazy. They never plant trees, and I presume never think of gardening.

Many thorn trees were to be seen as we journeyed on, and the dragoman told us that the crown of thorns which was placed upon the head of our Savior is supposed to have been made with thorns taken from the trees which grow there. Such long, pointed thorns! Oh, how sad to think of the tender flesh being pierced by them! Jesus was scourged,—severely whipped. That ought to have been enough suffering; but here came the soldiers with a platted crown of thorns, and placed it upon the tender head. Still not enough; he was nailed to a cross and then his side was pierced with a spear. Oh, what agony! The cup of sorrow was full. Christ drank it, and the will of the Lord was done. Children, do you know he died for you? Yes, for all of us. He has left us many good instructions and among them is this, "Pray that ye enter not into temptation."

As we neared the Dead Sea the country grew more barren looking. The ground in places was covered with salt and sulphur. No flowers were growing there, and not a bird could be seen flying around, so we pronounced it a desolate place because no living thing was in sight. If you look at the picture closely you may see a few small pieces of wood upon the ground, but not a blade of grass. I imagine those large sticks which stand together are intended to have canvas thrown over them to be used by bathers, for travelers often bathe in the Dead Sea just for the novelty of it. Owing to the rain which fell fast the day we were there, not any of our party ventured in. We did not tarry very long, for there was but little pleasure in being at such a desolate place.

The Arab who kept close to my side, so that assistance might be given when needed, did not ride a horse or donkey, but walked every step of the way. Arabs are the greatest fellows to walk I ever heard of, and they never seemed one bit tired when night came. The boy usually kept up with the horse, but occasionally he would hurry back, and at such times I heard him pounding something. My curiosity was at last aroused, and on looking back I beheld him hammering a piece of hard bread and breaking it in tiny little pieces. Now you may think we were sorry for the poor fellow, and that day instead of eating luscious oranges for luncheon we gave them to him. It was surprising to know how quickly they disappeared. After eating them he said, "Me very good donkey boy; backsheesh." We had orders not to give money, or anything else, to the servants, because they would give us trouble with their continual begging. We found there was some truth in the matter, so from that time on nothing more was given them.

The wind was blowing hard the day we saw the Dead Sea and the heavy water was in commotion. The waves rolled on the shore making quite a roaring sound. The wa-

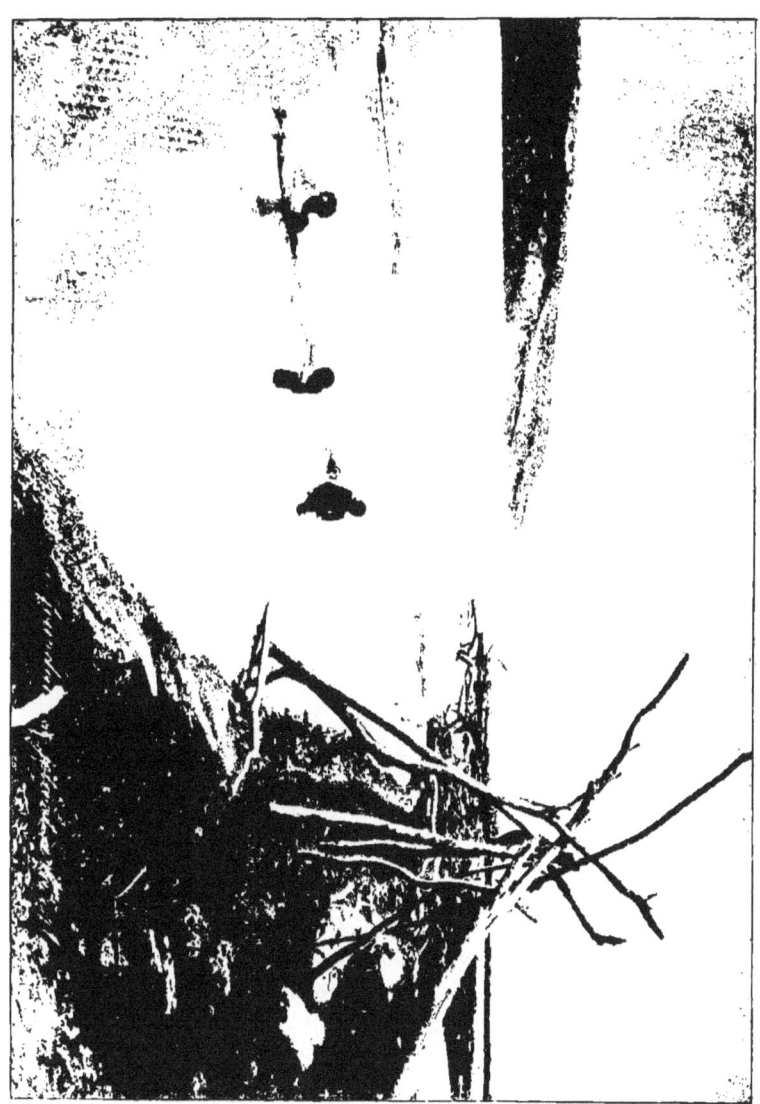

Men Bathing in Dead Sea.

ter is intensely bitter and salty, and after having tasted some of it I felt sorry enough, for the bitter taste was in my mouth the rest of the day, and even now I almost shudder when thinking of it.

You know this body of water is spoken of in Scripture as the "salt sea," "the sea of the plain" and the "east sea." Not a fish is found in its waters and the name Dead Sea seems fitting, for it is death to animal life.

A ride of perhaps four miles brought us to the banks of the river Jordan, and there we dismounted and ate our luncheon. Oh what a relief to be upon our feet again and then to be under the shade of trees. The contrast between this resting place and the last one was great, for there everything was dead; here were green grass and beautiful trees.

Do you remember the Bible story of John the Baptist who preached in the wilderness of Judea? You know great crowds of people went from all parts of the country to hear him, for he told them something they had never heard before. This man was very poor and wore the coarsest kind of clothing, which was camel's hair, "and a leathern girdle about his loins." He ate the simplest kind of food, consisting of locusts and wild honey. Though poor his ministry was successful, and many people confessed their sins and went down into the water and were "baptized of him in Jordan," the very river on whose banks we ate our noonday lunch. The people wondered "whether he was the Christ or not," and John, not desiring to receive any more reverence than belonged to him, said to the people, "He that cometh after me is mightier than I, whose shoes I am not worthy to bear." In time Jesus appeared and desired baptism, but John felt too unworthy to baptize such a personage as Jesus, so refused to administer it, saying, "I have need to be baptized of thee, and comest thou to me?" Well, they talked the matter over and the Savior said, "Suffer it to be so now," and the good preacher complied with the wish; after which John and Jesus came "up straightway out of the water: and, lo, the heavens were opened unto him, and he saw the spirit of God descending like a dove, and lighting upon him."

The Jordan is mentioned many times in the Scriptures, and we feel that every part of it is sacred. We cannot tell where John baptized the blessed Master, or where Elisha told Naaman to wash seven times that he might be healed of the leprosy, but we do know that the river Jordan which we saw is the same river in which John baptized Jesus and a great multitude of people.

The name of no other river is known so far away as that of the Jordan. And why should not Christians of all ages love to read and talk about it? Thousands of Christians all over the world, and of every nation, have made pilgrimages to Palestine expressly to stand on the banks of the river, or, better yet, to bathe in its waters. It was enough for us to stand on its banks, to see the trees in full leaf, and to sit upon the beautiful green grass and partake of the good things of earth.

River Jordan.

The picture which you see is a good representation of the river, and unless you view the stream itself you will never see a more perfect picture.

We left the banks of the sacred stream after luncheon and rode back to our camp at Jericho. While riding along the Arab guards entertained us by showing how wonderfully well they managed their horses. A motion of the hand gave the horse to understand that a circle was to be made, and with surprise we watched them make it. The horse and rider understood each other well.

Our dragoman joined in the ride, and it seemed an easy matter for him to outride his Arab friends. He had a swift-footed Arabian horse, and at times it seemed that its feet scarcely touched the grass as it moved along. A gentleman of our party joined the ride, and it was plain to see that he was not used to managing a horse as well as the rest.

When near a small village women were seen carrying upon their heads great stacks of wood and brush. What drudges! we thought; and while watching them walk along we wondered whether the poor creatures ever became discouraged with their lot, whether they would be willing to exchange the life of drudgery for one of comfort and ease if a way were opened to them. Down deep in my heart I felt wonderfully blessed in being allowed to live in a land where women are on an equality with men and not beneath them, as is the case in Palestine.

On reaching camp in the evening the dragoman informed us that we had ridden twenty-four miles during that day. You may well imagine we were surprised to hear it, and you may know we were exceedingly tired and anxious for rest. Two nights were spent at the same camping place, but the dragoman said we should take a long ride the next day; consequently all must arise early in the morning. Sweet sleep did not come to me that night and there was no chance to nap in the morning, for the tin can pounding and bell ringing aroused us at four o'clock. Oh, what a noise! Wedding serenaders in the country are the only ones who are able to make music to compare with it. Quickly we arose and hastily dressed, then made our way to the dining tent; and while we partook of the morning meal our tents were taken down and packed upon the back of mules and donkeys. There they stood, loaded with camp fixtures, and before the camp ground was vacated cook stove, bed and bedding and large boxes of dishes, and victuals were all packed for the journey. The order to mount our horses was given, and as soon as possible we were upon their backs.

Camp had been at the foot of the mountain, so up, up, up we went, right from the start. The roads were in a terrible condition, and sometimes it seemed almost impossible to cross the deep gullies which the water had washed in them.

Three servants accompanied us now instead of one, as heretofore,—Yosef, Mustaff, and an Abyssinian who was extremely black. These three kept very close to us while riding along, so that assistance might be rendered when desired. I have a distinct recollection of seeing some very large holes in the road, which the servants were compelled to fill with stones while we were waiting, so that we might pass over. I also call to mind times when one of the men led the ladies' horses while the second one held them on, and very carefully did the trusty animals step until over those dangerous places. The gentlemen of the party received help too; but one servant was all that was needed, for there was no chance for them to slip off of the back of their horses.

We were in the saddle long before sunrise, and after riding an hour or more the top of the first hill was reached and a short stop made. In looking back we saw the sun coming from behind Mount Nebo; and oh what a beautiful picture of the Dead Sea and the winding Jordan! Time was too precious to be spent in looking long at one picture, so we rode on, and that day proved to be the most trying day's ride of the whole twenty-one.

CHAPTER IX.

Strange Kind of Fuel.—The Village Oven.—Women's Work.—Fresh Bread. — The Little Baby. — Landmarks. — Bethel.— My Faithful Friend.—A Trying Time in the Saddle.—Sinjal.

IN some towns and villages wood is very scarce and the fuel consists of grass and dried manure. When riding through a village one day we noticed something sticking against the low stone wall, and we naturally wondered what the strange decoration could be. On getting near the wall, to our utter surprise, we found it to be manure which women had made into cakes and placed there to dry. Some day it would be cast into the oven with the bunches of grass.

In our Savior's time grass was burned; for we read, "Wherefore, if God so clothe the grass of the field, which to day is, and to morrow is cast into the oven, shall he not much more clothe you, O ye of little faith?"

The village oven was rather odd looking, being shaped very much like a large jug. There was an opening near the ground for fire, and a hole in the top for the escape of smoke.

When bread is made by mixing flour and water into a thin batter, it is baked by being poured on the outside of a heated oven. This makes thin, wafer-like cakes. But when a stiff dough is made it is baked between two fires made of manure; and when baked in that way it is said the smell of manure is noticeable. We did not tarry long in that village, therefore escaped tasting the vile stuff called bread.

Baking seems to have been women's work ages ago, for we have an account of Samuel telling the Israelites what they might expect if a new king reigned over them, as they greatly desired. After enumerating many things, Samuel said, "And he will take your daughters to be confectionaries, and to be cooks, and to be bakers." Then we read how "two women shall be grinding at the mill, the one shall be taken, and the other left." Grinding flour in small stone mills daily was woman's work, and making bread followed immediately after. But I have written enough to show that what we saw corresponded well with Bible accounts; and it greatly strengthened our belief in the Book of books.

When we started from Jerusalem there was bread enough taken along to supply our wants till the city of Nazareth was reached; but by that time it was not only very stale, but mouldy too. When the fresh supply was given us you may be sure it was welcome. Our bread was baked in the city oven and wood used for fuel. There may have been plenty of dirt in the flour, but I am very sure there was no odor of manure about the bread.

While riding from one camping place to another we passed very large grain fields which were beautifully green. In one of those fields I remember having seen three persons—man, woman and baby—and they were one family.

The mother was working hard pulling weeds out of the grain and the father—lazy man that he was—rocked the baby; for it was in a little homemade hammock. Two sticks had been pounded in the ground; to them the baby's cradle had been fastened, and it took but a slight movement to send the little one back and forth,—a very easy task for one so strong. And we thought the man would feel ashamed to have strangers see him sitting there employed in that kind of work. But—do you know?—instead of being ashamed he seemed pleased.

Fences are not seen in Palestine, but the limit of each man's land is known by what is called a landmark. It usually consists of a heap of stones placed at the corner of the owner's land. Persons passing through fields are not always aware whose land they are passing over. Especially is it so if you are a stranger in the country. You know Ruth was a stranger in and around Bethlehem; and when she had permission from Naomi to go and gather ears of corn she happened to get "on a part of the field belonging unto Boaz."

There are dishonest people all over the world. In the Bible we read of such characters, and we come to a passage like this: "Some remove the landmarks; they violently take away flocks, and feed thereof." You see the heap of stones is taken away and nothing is left to mark the boundary line.

At noon we lunched in the ruins of an old church in Bethel. There is where Abram and Lot stopped after leaving Mesopotamia. "And there he builded an altar unto the Lord, and called upon the name of the Lord." "And Esau hated Jacob because of the blessing wherewith his father blessed him." To get away from the angry brother, Jacob fled from home. After traveling until tired and weary, he found a resting place. The sun was set, so Jacob concluded to remain where he was during the night. He had no bed, or pillow either; but "he took of the stones of that place and put them for his pillows, and lay down in this place to sleep." He had a wonderful dream; and possibly you may call it to mind. Then Jacob was afraid; so he "rose up early in the morning, and took the stone that he had put for his pillows, and set it up for a pillar, and he called the name of that place Bethel."

Bethel was a poor village on a hill; the people were half naked, hungry looking creatures, and it seemed to me that all the men and boys of the village had made it a point to be in the ruins of the church that day. My luncheon was not enjoyed, for the sight of those hungry people took away my appetite. The dragoman did not offer them anything, for no doubt he decided it was utterly impossible to furnish food for hungry tourists and a village full of people besides. A bone was thrown to a dog which stood looking on; but the poor fellow lost it, for a gray-bearded Arab caught the animal, took it from him, and without one bit of embarrassment undertook the task of gnawing that bone himself. The dog showed signs of resentment, but no account was kept of that, so the bone was never returned.

The people there are a lazy set, and they almost starve. No attention is paid to farming or gardening, consequently food is scarce and clothing scant. I never waste sympathy on full-grown lazy people; but the poor, half-starved looking children and dogs I felt sorry for.

After resting a while at this place the order was given to move on, and very soon after we were on the road traveling wearily along. My horse was a very gentle animal, and I had a kindly feeling in my heart for him. Horses in that country get along without a name; but I proposed *my* faithful friend should have one, so I called him "John." He was not a beautiful animal; oh, no! Really, he was the ugliest animal in the company; but I didn't care. His ears were short—looked as though they had been nipped with frost; then, in addition to that, they had slits cut in them— a distinguishing mark which his master had given him— and I, like his master, could always tell John from all the other horses. If by accident some one had taken him, I was sure to be unhappy till he was returned.

John and I got along real well. He didn't care to trot along briskly, and I was very willing to let him do as he pleased in the matter. Well, to tell the truth, children, I was cowardly, and fast riding made me feel as though I was going to fall right off. Now, I hadn't one bit of a desire to get off of John's back suddenly, and the very thought of such a thing scared me; so we moved along in a lazy sort of a way. Occasionally a servant thought he would put some life in John by using a club; but I allowed no interference. We suited each other exactly, and I'm quite sure John missed me when the last day's ride was ended.

My saddle was a real good English sidesaddle, but, unfortunately for me, it continually slipped out of position on the horse's back. At first thought it seemed to need tightening up; but after doing so several times we found that kind of doctoring proved to be of little account; for every time I took my position over went the saddle again. There was but little enjoyment in the ride that day, for my time was spent in trying to sit erect upon the horse's back. Hour after hour my distress increased, until it seemed hardly possible to ride longer. The continued strain weakened my back so that I could scarcely sit up. Walking would have been a pleasure; but such a thing was out of the question, for the company would ride faster than I could walk, and so leave me far behind.

The day was far spent and it was drawing on toward sundown. Camp, they said, was not many miles away. Oh, how we wished it was only a few steps; but on we rode, with a strong desire to get to the place of rest as soon as possible.

The company was somewhat divided that day. Some of them were away on ahead of us, and a few were quite a little distance behind. The road was very narrow, and so it was necessary to ride single file. There were rocks of all sizes in the road, and some measuring five or six feet in width lying just outside of the path. When only a few feet away from one of them my strength gave way, and the back which had served me so well all day refused to be tried any longer. Near by was my husband, and with trembling voice I said to him, "Please help me, or I shall surely fall, for I'm unable to sit here longer." He sprang to my side, and just in time to keep me from falling from the horse's back. Those great flat rocks came in use now, for my husband placed me upon one of them, and for a while I lay there with my face down. "Oh, what shall we do if I can ride no further?" I thought, "and so far from home and friends." Ah, home never seemed dearer than then; and, children, I was foolish enough to shed tears. But I want to tell you it doesn't pay to shed tears. It does not show bravery, and when sorely tried one needs to brace up. I brushed my tears away and took fresh courage; and let me tell you the Lord helped me do it.

Our horses were anxious to get to their resting place, so quietly they walked on. The ladies and gentlemen who were riding behind came along one by one, passing us on their way to camp, and they carried word that "Mrs. Miller has fainted." After resting a while we left the rock and together walked on to camp. When almost there the dragoman met us saying, "I was just on my way to bring you in."

You can imagine how glad we were when camp was reached, for there stood the tents, and there was the place of rest. The beds had been made nicely and I found rest upon one of them. Shall I ever forget that experience while passing through the Holy Land? I think not.

"How could you stand such a journey?" has been asked me time and again, and as many times have I answered, "The Lord gave me strength according as I needed it;" for I was unused to hardships and not any stronger than the majority of women. It is quite necessary on a journey like that to be patient, uncomplaining and not fretful, and the Lord is able to give us that kind of a disposition if we call upon him. Many of us would have turned back to Jerusalem willingly, but there was no such thing as going back after having once started. Onward was the cry, and if sickness came upon us we were carried along. If death should be the lot of any one a grave by the roadside would be the last resting place. Such graves were passed, and how sad we felt at the thought of some lonely pilgrim having been laid by the roadside.

Each day some one of the women felt it almost impossible to go further; but it made no difference, they rode on and on, murmuring not in the least.

I told you the roads were in a dreadful condition. The stones were so plentiful it was hard work to see the path much of the way. The horses walked with noses down, smelling as they walked along. In that way they found there truly was a path, and that other horses had gone over the same rocks.

Many of the party had falls from their horses, but no one was hurt. All were so tired they scarcely knew what to do; but I was the only one who had given out. We had traveled thirty-four miles during that day and had been in the saddle almost eleven hours.

Sinjal is the name of an Arab village, and on a high hill near by our tents were pitched that night. Owing to the fact that I was worn out, I saw nothing of the people or village.

We were up the next morning early, not entirely rested; indeed, very far from it; but when ready to mount our horses I was delighted to find the saddle had been adjusted satisfactorily, thanks to my husband, who had insisted upon a change that I might not be compelled to ride in such misery another eleven hours. The fault lay in John; his back was not suited to the saddle, and the lack of flesh was supplied with padding; and ever after that I rode comfortably and never became exhausted again. All that day I was not able to guide my horse, because of extreme weakness; but faithful Yosef led John, and silently we went on.

CHAPTER X.

Shiloh.—Jacob's Well.—Tomb of Joseph.—Shechem.— Samaria.—Gibeah. —Dothan in the Distance.—Fountain of Gideon.—Shunem.— Shunammite's Son.—Nain.

THE country through which we passed was less stony, and the roads were more smooth and level. Horses and riders seemed glad for the change and enjoyed it immensely. Land was under better cultivation, for olive and fig trees were there, and everywhere were signs of thrift.

When camp was reached a distance of twenty-two miles had been traveled. The tents were pitched at Shechem, but we took the road which leads to the old city of Shiloh, where a heap of ruins with broken columns was seen. Far back in history interesting things are told about Shiloh, for it was one of the foremost places of the Old World.

The children of Israel set up a tabernacle there. Several of the tribes had not received their inheritance. At the suggestion of Joshua three men from each tribe were chosen and sent out to describe the land; and on their return with the description "Joshua cast lots for them in Shiloh before the Lord: and there Joshua divided the land unto the children of Israel according to their division."

The ark of the Lord rested at Shiloh many years. Now the ark of the Lord was the sacred chest which held the tables of the law, and while it was there feasts were held annually, and the people worshiped and offered sacrifice unto the Lord.

Not far from Shiloh lived a man whose name was Elkanah; and yearly both he and his good wife Hannah went to "worship and sacrifice unto the Lord of hosts." Hannah grieved because she had neither sons nor daughters, and when they went to Shiloh to sacrifice she prayed long and fervently to the Lord, saying, "I will give him unto the Lord all the days of his life."

Well, time rolled on and Hannah's prayer was answered; the Lord gave a little son to the faithful woman, and she called him Samuel, "because I have asked him of the Lord." The promise made by the mother long before had not been forgotten, and as soon as the child was old enough Hannah took little Samuel away to Shiloh and gave him to Eli, the high priest, saying, "I have lent him to the Lord; and he worshiped the Lord there." Children, don't you think the mother felt lonely going back to her home without the bright, prattling little fellow? Surely she missed him, but not a word of complaint was uttered. She said, however, "My heart rejoiceth in the Lord." Oh, how she praised the Lord, and her song of thanksgiving was long. I would like to tell you about Eli, who judged Israel forty years, and who, through neglect of duty in the raising of his sons, had to suffer the consequences; but it is time to leave the ruined city and go on toward our lunching place, which was at "Jacob's well." There were no trees to shelter us from the noonday sun, so those who had umbrellas made use of them. All Christian people think of Jacob's well as being a sacred place, and we could not help but think of the Bible characters who once stood where we were then resting. Our mind went back to the time when Jesus was there, sitting upon the rim of the well and talking to the woman who had come to draw water.

Jesus had been to Jerusalem during the passover season, and while there had found men who were selling sheep, oxen and doves in the temple. Such desecration could not be tolerated, so he chased them all out; and after giving them some good lessons he journeyed on toward Galilee. He was weary from the long journey, and while his disciples went to the city to buy something to eat he sat and rested. Even though tired he did not fail to teach the Samaritan woman some good lessons. There he told her of the water of eternal life; and there he revealed himself unto her, saying, "I that speak unto thee am he." Jesus had a message for the Samaritans, and the woman carried it to them. At first it was hard to understand what Jesus meant. She pointed to the mountain which was not far away and said, "Our fathers worshiped in this mountain: and ye say, that in Jerusalem is the place where men ought to worship." But Jesus showed her plainly what he desired, and without waiting for the water pot, she went into the city and told what Jesus had said to her. Many went to see him; they insisted upon Jesus staying with them, and he was there two days. Before he left "many more believed because of his own word."

A church was built over the well many years ago, but nothing is to be seen of it now. An arch which at one time covered it had broken away, and through the opening a descent of several feet was made, when the mouth of Jacob's well was reached. The company desired to taste the water, so by the help of Arabs who stood by, and with the use of pieces of rope tied together and fastened to an old can, their wish was gratified and each one tasted water from the well which had been dug in Bible times.

The time of resting ended, and Jacob's well was left behind. Our next stop was to be made at the tomb of Joseph, supposed to be the real burial place of Jacob's favorite son. The story of Joseph's life is extremely interesting, and I should take great pleasure in telling it to you, but space forbids. The time came for the good man to die, and the cares and toils of life ended. His body was embalmed—as was the custom of the country—and placed in a coffin. "And the bones of Joseph, which the children of Israel brought up out of Egypt, buried they in Shechem."

When the famine was great in the land where Joseph's father and brethren dwelt, he was greatly concerned; and when the brethren asked for corn after their arrival in Egypt it was not withheld from them, even when Joseph had power to do so. Prosperity had not closed this good man's heart against home folks, though he had been shamefully treated by them. I think a lesson of love may be learned, for hatred was far from his heart, and in every action love was made manifest.

We rode on from Joseph's tomb until the valley of Shechem was entered. There we were between two mountains,—Gerizim, where the blessing of obedience was pronounced, and Ebal, where cursings upon the rebellious were made known.

Our camping place was at the foot of the mountains, and while some of the party with the dragoman made the ascent of Gerizim others went on to camp. Mr. Heilpin informed us that the ascent of the mountain would be rather a hard one, so we that were tired preferred going on to camp; therefore only a few of the company undertook the climb. The tents were pitched on a piece of level ground beneath the steep ascent of Gerizim, and only a short distance from the city of Nablus.

In Bible times the city went by the name of Sichem or Shechem. It was the chief city of the Samaritans for years and years, because of the temple which was erected on Mount Gerizim. There are still a few Samaritans in Nablus, and it is said that at certain times of the year they go to Gerizim and offer sacrifices as did their fathers before them. There is no temple for them to worship in now, for it was destroyed ever so many years ago.

Abram knew something about Shechem, too, for it was there that he made his first stop after leaving Haran; and there he built an altar. Shechem was also known as a city of refuge in Bible times. You see the Lord told Joshua to tell the children of Israel to appoint cities of refuge. Any one who had been unfortunate enough to accidentally kill a man could, by fleeing thither and getting inside the gates, find safety from his pursuers. Several cities were appointed for that purpose, and Shechem was one of the number.

Nablus is quite a large city, and a very dirty one, too. The houses are built of stone and the streets are very narrow. A great many soap factories were there, and many heaps of ashes could be seen outside the city. Lepers are there, and many of them, too,—poor, afflicted creatures. We were fortunate to escape seeing them, as they did not happen to get where we were.

Wherever we camped men, women and children of the cities flocked to see us, and Nablus was no exception to the rule. Curiously they watched every movement, and no doubt were highly entertained. Sometimes it was quite annoying to us, yet we were pleased to know insults were never offered.

It was almost dark when the company who had gone up the mountain returned. Shortly after the call for dinner,—the evening meal,—was given, and gladly did we all respond. One hour was usually spent at a meal, and only a short time passed between it and the time of retiring, and we were always as glad to go to our little beds as to eat a meal.

The next morning at seven o'clock we left Shechem, going toward Samaria. By this time I was able to ride with ease and comfort, for I had rested from the extreme fatigue of a few days before. We rode through the beautiful green valleys and enjoyed it very much. The saddle kept to its place upon the horse's back, and riding was a pleasure instead of a dread.

Samaria is a small, dirty village now, and hedges of cactus surround it. Ruins seem to tell the story of the grandeur of former years, as we read that "Samaria shall become desolate: for she hath rebelled against her God." The city had been built by a king whose name was Omri, who reigned over Israel twelve years; then he died and was buried in Samaria. Omri was a very bad man and his wickedness was worse than that of the kings who had ruled before him. He had a son whose name was Ahab, and for twenty-two years he ruled Israel. Having had a bad example set him by his father, and being no doubt wicked by nature, it was not hard for Ahab to go on in wickedness; so he "reared an altar for Baal in the house of Baal, which was in Samaria." You see the city was the seat of idol worship, and a good place to do mission work; so Philip undertook the task and preached Christ to them, and the people "all gave heed, from the least to the greatest."

There was not time for a lengthy stay at Samaria, so we journeyed on. Olive groves, fig orchards and almond trees were seen over the valley and the hillside, with here and there barley fields.

Noon drew near, and we stopped at a place supposed to be Gibeah, and there we ate lunch, in a fine old olive grove whose trees were a protection for us; and for two hours we rested, sheltered from the hot sun.

We left Gibeah, and rode on into a broad valley. A mountain was seen far away to the north, and they called it Mount Hermon. With the aid of our field glass snow was seen upon it, and an Australian lady of the party seemed glad to know there was a possibility of getting where snow really was, for, said she, "I never saw snow in my life."

Dothan was in the distance, too, and you know that is the place where Joseph went to seek his brethren, and where they sold him to the company of Ishmaelites. Everywhere you look the eye falls upon places which are familiar to the Bible reader. There in view were the mountains of Gilboa where Saul and Jonathan were slain, and there, too, was Mount Carmel, the home of the prophet.

We descended a steep, rocky road into a valley again, and passed a Bedouin camp on the way. Only a short time passed when we were made to rejoice at the sight of our tents, the only home we had. A twenty-eight mile ride in one day was a tiresome piece of work, and when we rode into camp and saw the tents it was truly a beautiful sight.

Early the next morning we were up and ready for a day's ride to Nazareth,—another hard day in the saddle. At the close of the day we found our tents pitched at Jenin. From there we rode on to the fountain of Gideon, which we found to be a nice, large fountain of pure, clear water coming out of a cave in the side of the mountain. One time the Lord told Gideon to take his army to that fountain and there he would try them for him. At first there were many thousand men; but the Lord said that only those who lapped water with their tongue, as a dog does, should go with Gideon. The men never knew they were to be tried that way; so they were sent down to the fountain, and some of them lapped the water, while others bowed down on their knees and drank. Those who lapped the water Gideon took and with them fought the Midianites, and Israel was saved by Gideon with only three hundred men.

We rode on directly to Jezreel. There Ahab had his home many years ago. No doubt in sight of where we were was the vineyard of Naboth which Ahab coveted.

Not very far from Jezreel is Sulem, the ancient Shunem of Bible times. It may have been a fine city then, but now it is a small village with a few huts inside of a cactus hedge. We rested and ate our noonday meal in the village. The touching story of the Shunammite woman came to our mind while there. We wondered where the house of the great woman with whom Elisha was constrained to eat bread was located. Elisha was a prophet who passed through the city often, and whenever it was convenient he rested at the house, and the woman and her husband felt themselves honored when called upon to entertain him. They knew he was a holy man, so decided to make a room for him on the wall, fitting it up with bed, table, stool and candlestick,—all of the conveniences,—so that when Elisha came around it would be found ready. Those people had a son whom they dearly loved. One time the boy went to his father in the field—just as little boys in this country sometimes do—and shortly after he was heard to say, "My head, my head." A lad carried him to his mother and "he sat on her knees till noon, and then died." She placed the lifeless body of her little boy upon the bed of Elisha, then closed the door, called her husband and said, "Send me, I pray thee, one of the young men, and one of the asses, that I may run to the man of God and come again." The husband was surprised to know she wanted to go to see the man of God then, never thinking, I suppose, that the beloved son had died. "It shall be well," was all she had time to say, and then, in a great hurry, she and the servant departed.

The prophet was found, and the sorrowful story related. What a journey the woman had in the burning sun, —for she went clear to Mount Carmel,—but a mother's love is enduring and unselfish. She thought only of the dear one, and having him brought to life again. At first the prophet thought to send Gehazi with his staff, but the woman would not hear to such a thing and refused to leave until Elisha "arose and followed her." All three of them went to the desolate home, and when the prophet was alone with the dead child he prayed to the Lord and put his mouth to the mouth of the child, and his hands upon the hands of the little one and warmed him up in that way. By and by the little boy sneezed, yes, seven times; then his eyes opened. The woman was called. "Then she went in and fell at his feet, and bowed herself to the ground, and took up her son, and went out." What a lesson of trust there is in this Bible story; and the Lord may be trusted these days just as well as then, if we only feel like doing so.

Our luncheon was eaten under lemon trees, but I believe there was not one bit of grass anywhere around us.

There were crowds of children who came out from the village to see us, and I wondered whether the Shunammite's son looked anything like those children. Their actions were very rude, and quite annoying to us, for almost continually they called out, "Backsheesh, backsheesh," and no matter how much backsheesh was given them they could not be persuaded to leave.

Backsheesh means a gift, and the inhabitants of that country expect all travelers to give them something. We had nothing but money for them, and each piece received had to be taken home, have a hole punched in it, and then strung on a string; after which they were tied around the forehead and worn as ornaments. Every time the head moved the coins jingled. Boys and girls were dressed alike, so it was hard to say who wore the money.

Some women were washing clothes at a fountain near the edge of the village, and I am sure you never saw any one wash as strangely as they. I do not know whether they used soap; anyway, the water did not indicate it. A garment was dipped in the water and made soaking wet. Then it was placed upon a large stone which was hollowed out a little. A small stone was held in the right hand, and with it the garment was pounded again and again. I saw nothing white in the wash, and indeed the colored pieces looked as though an extra rubbing was needed, even after they had been pounded and rolled again and again.

Shunem was rather cleaner looking than most of the villages passed through, and yet there was room for improvement, for great piles of manure and filth were seen on the main streets, which looked as though they had been there for ages. Children were perched upon the filth, sitting there as comfortably as could be imagined. Vermin were thick, causing much uneasiness to both tourist and Arab. A woman decided to make money by showing a plump baby which she carried upon her arm. Meekly she said, "Backsheesh for baba;" and we responded to the request, giving a few coins, then turning away from her. In a short time after a half-grown girl presented herself before us with the same plump baby, and with the same request. No doubt the woman thought showing her baby was paying business; therefore placed the child in the hands of others to help along the enterprise. Finally the time came for us to leave Shunem, and real glad we were to get away.

Nain comes next in our line of travel, and possibly you remember it as being the place to which Jesus and many of his disciples went. As they neared the gate of the city a dead man was carried out. He was the only son of a widow, and no doubt her only support. The Lord was sorry for the bereaved mother and said, "Weep not." Jesus touched the bier and told the young man to arise. "And he that was dead sat up, and began to speak; and he delivered him to his mother." The city of Nain was once prosperous, but now only a few miserable houses are to be seen.

It was getting on toward sundown as we rode up a steep hill, and when the top was reached the city of Nazareth was in full view. Every one of the party seemed anxious to reach camp, and the horses were urged to a faster pace. During the day some of the party had unpleasant experiences. A German lady who rode well was thrown from her horse, and striking a stone, bruised her face. Another lady was riding along rather unconcerned, when her horse decided to rest himself. Forthwith he got down in a great mud puddle, while the lady was still seated upon his back. Indeed, scarcely a day passed but some one of the party had a fall; but I am glad to say that husband and I kept upon the horses' backs, and our horses kept upon their feet all the way. So we never had a fall.

CHAPTER XI.

Riding into Nazareth.—Virgin's Fountain.—Tricky Horses.—Cana of Galilee.—Tiberias.—Story of Jesus and his Disciples.—Boat Ride on the Sea of Galilee.—Capernaum. — Mounting Horses.—Disappearance of the Dragoman.—A Serious Accident.—Lake Huleh.—Cesarea Philippi.—Mount Hermon.—Crossing the River Pharpar.—Damascus.—Via Recta.—Bible References to Courts.—Cup of Coffee.— Water Seller.

WITH the dragoman heading the company we rode into Nazareth single file just as the sun went down. He seemed delighted to be leader of such a large party of tourists, and as we marched along the people looked amazed at the turnout. Our stay at this place was longer than at any of the preceding places, for reaching there Saturday evening gave us Sunday as an extra day of rest, as on that day no traveling was done.

Our tents were pitched near the "Virgin's Fountain," which is considered one of the holy places of the city, because it is thought that Mary, the mother of Jesus, was in the habit of going there for water. We took pleasure in watching the women fill their large jars, which held perhaps three gallons of water. Mothers with tiny babies upon their arms went to the fountain, and young, laughing girls mingled with the crowd. Some of them were in a hurry, while many stopped long enough to have a pleasant chat and tell a bit of news. One would naturally suppose a jar holding three gallons of water would be a heavy burden to carry; but the women helped each other place them upon the head, after which the individual walked off unconcerned, seemingly not having a fear as to the vessel tumbling off. The bearing of water seemed to be one of the burdens placed upon the women of that country, and they bore it cheerfully. Not a man was to be seen carrying the smallest vessel. It was the custom for women to carry water in Abraham's time, for we read that when a servant was sent to seek a wife for Isaac, and a certain city was reached, "he made his camels to kneel down without the city by a well of water at the time of the evening, even the time that women go out to draw water."

The Sabbath Day was not spent resting in our tents, for we had too strong a desire to see something of the "city of Jesus." No doubt you remember that Mary and Joseph had their home in Nazareth before going up to Bethlehem to be taxed; but the Nazareth of Joseph and Mary's time is not the Nazareth we looked upon, for since then battles have been fought there, and the city destroyed several times. It has been rebuilt, however, and each time the original site was used. The natives were bright-faced and rather neatly dressed, and the contrast between this city and others was great. We were not surprised to learn that Protestantism had a hold there, and that solved the mystery.

Nazareth is built on the side of a hill and presented quite a beautiful appearance. Upon one of the hills which surround the city is an orphanage school for girls, which, we learned, was under the care of a self-sacrificing woman. Early in life she left parents, home and friends, went to Nazareth and took charge of the little girls who lived there, teaching them the way to Christ. At first it may have seemed a thankless task, but to-day it is plainly seen that her labors were not in vain. An English society supplied her with funds. All money given for the support of such institutions in a foreign land is well spent.

There is a Protestant church in Nazareth, and we attended services there. Two ministers of the Church of England conducted the services, and the story of the Shunammite woman was read to us. The preachers belonged to our party; the congregation was made up mostly of tourists, and a small company it was.

The first thirty years of Jesus' life were spent in Nazareth; but "he did not many mighty works there, because of their unbelief." Jesus talked very plainly to the people, and they were filled with wrath and "rose up and thrust him out of the city, and led him unto the brow of the hill whereon their city was built, that they might cast him down headlong. But he, passing through the midst of them, went his way." The mount of precipitation is shown the traveler, and we tried to imagine how the people appeared when Christ deliberately walked away from them.

We spent a restful day at Nazareth, which helped us to bear the journey of the following week. Our hearts were filled with gratitude to the Lord, and on bended knees we thanked him for the great privilege of being permitted to see the city of the meek and lowly Nazarene.

One hundred and seventy-two miles had been traveled from the time we mounted our horses at Jerusalem up to the time Nazareth was reached, and every mile of the way was traveled on horseback. It is hard to tell how much suffering many of the poor horses endured, for the condition of their backs was distressing. Only two out of the eighteen were in good condition, and we two rode them. Some of the saddles fitted the horses' backs poorly, and that caused the skin to rub off, which created a large sore place. When the hostlers removed the saddles in the evening our sympathies were aroused, for never before had we seen anything to equal the raw state of those horses' backs. The men did not fancy having spectators, and their faces indicated their displeasure; but we looked anyway, and left when it suited us. The Arabs may have neglected to give the animals proper care and attention, thus helping the sore to grow larger and more inflamed. If the men had been less idle and more attentive probably the faithful animals would have been in better trim for traveling. Some of the horses were a little tricky, for they had a habit of rolling. No matter whether on a smooth road or in a mud puddle, when the desire to roll came to them down they went, and the patience of the ladies was sorely tried, for they were sure to be upon the animals' backs. The riders never thought it a funny thing for them to do, but those who looked on naturally smiled.

Sunday's rest at Nazareth was quite a benefit to us, and Monday morning we were up early, ready for the onward march.

As we rode out of camp, the Virgin's Fountain was again passed, and once more we saw the water carriers busy. Bidding adieu to Nazareth we rode up a steep hill, and looking back saw the white houses as they stood in the bright sunlight. The last look was taken, and we passed over the brow of the hill, feeling sure that the city of Jesus would be seen no more by us.

Kefr Kenna is a small village through which we passed, and where a short stop was made. For centuries it was thought to be Cana of Galilee, where, in the time of Christ, there was a marriage. You remember that Jesus, his mother and the disciples were there. "And when they wanted wine, the mother of Jesus saith unto him, They have no wine." Well, Jesus didn't seem quite ready to perform a miracle when his mother spoke to him, and his reply was, "Mine hour is not yet come." But no doubt the mother felt his hour had come, so she told the servants to do whatever Jesus instructed them to do. "Then Jesus saith unto them, Fill the water pots with water. And they filled them up to the brim." When the order to draw out the water was given, lo, there was wine, and the governor drank of it, speaking words of praise, for it was even better than the first which had been passed; so at this place Jesus began to perform miracles.

Two immense stone jars were shown us, said to be the very jars our Savior used at that marriage; but we do not vouch for the truth of the statement.

There was very little to interest us in Cana, therefore our stay was short, and we rode on toward Tiberias, reaching there in time to eat our noonday meal.

Tiberias is by the Sea of Galilee and was once the capital of Galilee; but, like other cities of Bible times, it had been destroyed. Not very many years ago the present city was partly destroyed by an earthquake, and the walls tell the story. There are hot springs at Tiberias, and it is said the water is too hot for immediate use. Many people who have rheumatism go there to bathe and be cured if possible. It is said the bath houses are filthy and abound in vermin; and, from what we saw of our boatmen, we concluded the private houses must be in as bad a condition as the bath houses.

The Sea of Galilee has another name which is, Lake of Gennesaret. On the shores of this body of water Jesus stood when the people pressed upon him, eager to hear the Word of God. And in our mind we saw the two empty ships at the time the crowd was so great Jesus decided to go aboard one of them, and asked Simon to push the boat from land. "And he sat down and taught the people out of the ship."

Fish are abundant in the lake now, just as they were in the time of Christ; for you remember Jesus said to Simon, "Launch out into the deep, and let down your nets for a draught." Simon had been out all night fishing, and had worked hard, but not a fish did he catch; and he felt there was poor pay in throwing out the nets again. So, after telling the Master of his ill luck, he said, "Nevertheless at thy word I will let down the net." And the result was "a great multitude of fishes." Then there was an accident, the net broke. "And they beckoned unto their partners, which were in the other ship, that they should come and help them. And they came and filled both the ships, so that they began to sink." The men were surprised to see so many fish, and were dreadfully alarmed, too, lest all should be lost; but "Jesus said unto Simon, Fear not; from henceforth thou shalt catch men."

The lake was liable to sudden storms, and not a ripple could be seen when boatmen started out from the shore; but soon the wind came down over the hills, and in a little while the water would be wonderfully disturbed. Just such a thing happened when Jesus asked his disciples to get in a boat and go before him to the other side of the sea. After the disciples left him "he departed into a mountain to pray." It was evening. Jesus was alone on land and the disciples were in their boats toiling away at the oars; "and about the fourth watch of the night he cometh unto them, walking upon the sea, and would have passed by them." Oh, how frightened all were, for they imagined the object to be a spirit, and it troubled them. But "immediately he talked with them, and saith unto them, Be of good cheer: it is I; be not afraid. And he went up unto them into the ship; and the wind ceased: and they were sore amazed in themselves beyond measure, and wondered." Then Peter thought he would like to try walking on the water, too. "But when he saw the wind boisterous, he was afraid; and beginning to sink, he cried, saying, Lord, save me!" Poor Peter had not faith enough to carry him through when the waves rolled around him; but "Jesus stretched forth his hand, and caught him, and said unto him, O thou of little faith, wherefore didst thou doubt?" Can you not imagine Christ standing with outstretched hands on the turbulent waters of Galilee? Then think of Peter on the verge of sinking. To-day Jesus stands ready to save all who call upon him.

Travelers usually have a strong desire to take a boat ride on the Sea of Galilee, and our company were as anxious as any who ever visited its shores. Arrangements were therefore made for a ride from Tiberias to Capernaum. Two boats, with the boatmen, were procured, and they were large enough to hold the party and rowers very nicely.

The men were strong, able-bodied fellows, and you will think so, too, when I tell you that each passenger was carried to the boats by them. You see, two of the boatmen put their hands together in such a manner as to form a seat, and we sat upon their hands as comfortably as you please, and kept from falling off by placing our arms about their necks. The water was not deep enough to reach our feet, so we got along very well. You may imagine the sight to have been amusing, for over half of the number weighed one hundred and seventy-five pounds apiece, and one old man almost tipped the scales at three hundred. The boatmen, no doubt, were anxious to place such burdens in the boat. The strong odor of fish was rather unpleasant, and it seemed best to close the eyes and thereby shut away the filthy condition of boat and men. The day was beautiful and the lake very smooth. The wind sometimes comes down over the hills, and as of old the result is a restless, uneasy sea. We were glad the water was not troubled that day.

The sun shone very hot, and when it struck the water its rays caused our eyes to smart. At the end of three hours Tell Hum was before us. After landing we walked up a hill through a rank growth of weeds higher than our heads, and there looked upon what is thought to be Capernaum, one of the chief cities of Palestine in Christ's time, where much of his time was spent in healing the sick and teaching the people. Jesus upbraided many cities for their neglect of duty, and Capernaum was among the number. Now read his warning words, "And thou, Capernaum, which art exalted unto heaven, shalt be brought down to hell: for if the mighty works, which have been done in thee, had been done in Sodom, it would have remained until this day. But I say unto you, That it shall be more tolerable for the land of Sodom in the day of judgment, than for thee."

The prophecy was fulfilled and all houses and churches were leveled to the ground. The hot sun shining upon the rank growth of weeds proved to be extremely disagreeable to us, therefore we shortened our stay. Entering the boats again, we were rowed to camp.

The tents were pitched near Magdala, about three miles from Tiberias, and our stopping place that night was only a few feet from the water, a beautiful looking place, but an extremely damp one. The gentlemen of the party took a good bath in the Sea of Galilee and pronounced it quite refreshing; the ladies were denied that privilege, for bathing dresses were too far away; so we missed that pleasure.

We retired rather late that night, but were quite willing to arise early the next morning, and by seven o'clock were in the saddle. Horseback riding was not so fatiguing now, and there really seemed to be a little pleasure in traveling over hill and plain.

I have told you about riding horseback, but you may not know how we mounted our horses. If plenty of rocks were to be found at the different stopping places mounting a horse was not so very hard; but many times the rocks were so small it would have taken hours and hours to throw them together to make a pile large enough for us to stand upon. No chairs, no rocks to stand on; then how did we mount? Well, the dragoman held out his hand and we put our foot upon it; then, after having placed one of our hands upon the horn of the saddle, we prepared to jump. Mr. Heilpin always said, "Ready? Now, one, two, three;" and by the time he had said three we were usually up in the saddle. But sometimes "three" was said, when no attempt had been made to jump; then one, two, three was repeated. Often our calculations and his counting failed to come out right; for we had forgotten to spring. Mounting the horses was real amusing, but awfully trying. Practice makes perfect, it has been said, and after a few lessons every one of the women was more active, and we mounted in a hurry.

While riding along one day we all lost sight of our dragoman, and it seemed quite strange to be without him. Yosef undertook to be our pilot, but as he became confused we concluded he answered the purpose but poorly; and the outlook to gain camp seemed rather uncertain. One of the party rode ahead and called out, "I'll take you through; follow me." We decided it was too much like the blind leading the blind, but just at that time the dragoman put in an appearance and we followed him. After riding a long distance a good resting place was found near a beautiful fountain. Each person used his own pleasure as to how the time should be spent. Some wrote letters and others took a nap. My time was spent in admiring the surroundings and reading a little. Every one seemed to enjoy the rest immensely, and when the call to leave was given we were loath to quit the spot.

Serious accidents sometimes happen to tourists, and I shall have to tell you of one which happened to one of our number. Just before the second call was given one of the ladies desired a switch, and as she stepped down to the place where they could be found her knee twisted and the bone snapped. Being near enough to hear it, I immediately went to her asking the question, "Are you hurt?" and the reply was, "Call the doctors;" which I did; and when the examination was made a serious break was announced. The doctors belonged to our party, but their medicines and instruments were at home. Servants were sent to camp in a gallop for bedstead, mattress and a board. The gentlemen made splints and gave their large white silk handkerchiefs for bandages. The bone was set and six men carried her to camp, and it was nine o'clock by the time we reached there.

The lady was of a very cheerful disposition, and therefore bore this misfortune uncomplainingly. I shall never forget that time, as a great gloom was cast over the company, and it seemed as though death had come into our midst.

Our camping place for that night was Ein-Baluka, and it seemed to be in the neighborhood of Bedouin Arabs, which fact was not pleasant to think of; but we got along all right and the watchful eye of the Lord was over us there, as well as at every other camping place. There was no other way for the lady to travel but by horseback, so a mattress was fastened upon the animal's back and Miss W. placed upon it, being tied there with sheets.

It looked very odd to see her riding backward, but there was no other way, for the broken limb had to be kept perfectly straight, as the least bit of a bend made it very painful. Her horse did not go out of a walk, yet there was a motion which caused the limb to roll. It was necessary to remedy that before going very far, and the lady said laughingly, "I'll fix something to hold it still," and forthwith a shawl-strap was brought forth. One end was placed about the afflicted limb, and the other end of the strap was held in her hand. That proved to be just the thing and saved much pain, because the foot was kept in its place.

Four days she was carried over the rough roads, crossing over Mount Hermon and the river Pharpar. A watchful eye was kept over the patient sufferer all of the way, and Arab men walked by her side to help when needed. In our line of march the company was headed by the dragoman, then Miss W. and the rest of us coming after, all riding single file.

One day a great marshy place was crossed, and as misfortunes don't come singly, it happened that Miss W.'s horse had to stick in the mud. Some of the gentlemen, with the help of an Arab, lifted the cripple from the horse and placed her upon the ground; after which the servants worked faithfully to extricate the animal. Considerable time was lost, but finally he was set free and we once more moved on.

Often such accidents happen when horses and donkeys are disabled; and as the owners of them can not take the animals over the mountain or remain to feed them the poor things must be left to suffer and finally die of starvation. My heart was made to ache for the animals which we saw by the roadside, unable to walk and left to die.

There were no more mishaps after this, and the crippled member was never heard to utter a complaint, and was the most cheerful one of the party. She was aware of the fact that the fracture would leave its results for life, but notwithstanding she was cheerful. If the lady could speak to you she would tell you her trust was in the One who watches over all of his children, for Miss W. was a Christian. When at home this lady was a diligent worker in the

Sunday school, and all along the journey she paid great attention to the noted Bible places, for, said she, "I shall tell it all to my class when I get home."

Children, did you ever think how much hard work your Sunday-school teachers do, that they may be able to show you the way to Christ? They are concerned about your soul's salvation, and many, many hours are anxiously spent in thinking and studying the best plan to present the Word of God to you Sunday after Sunday. Oh do not pass the truths by thoughtlessly, for remember that your reward in the end will be meted out according to the opportunity you had of learning the right.

We are getting on toward the end of our journey, and this time we find the tents pitched at Lake Huleh, better known, perhaps, as the "Waters of Merom."

During the day Bedouin Arab camps were passed, and we saw their tents, which were made of goats' hair closely woven together, making them water-tight. Plenty of fish are found in the waters of Lake Huleh, and Bedouin Arabs go there to fish and hunt. These people are of a roving nature, therefore remain but a short time at one place. Their families go with them, of course, and that means the donkeys, camels, sheep and goats. As long as pasture is green, they stay at one place, only moving when pasture becomes scarce.

I wonder how many of you ever saw a buffalo. Well, we saw a few of them on the low ground at the head of the lake. They were very small compared with those of the western plains of this country; they seemed to be gentle and were not disturbed at all by our company passing by.

The next camping place was at the base of Mount Hermon, whose top was capped with snow. Not far from the tents springs of water gushed out from beneath the rocks. Just beyond the springs was a large cave, where people went to worship a god called "Pan."

The country through which we traveled that day was beautiful. Plenty of green grass was to be seen, and olive groves were all around us. We crossed an old Roman bridge, and found our canvas homes in an olive grove which had a stream of clear mountain water flowing through it.

The situation of Banias was beautiful on the side of the mountain, with ravines and sparkling streams of water about it. Only a few houses were in the village, and not much of interest was to be seen there; but wherever we went while passing through Palestine Jesus and his disciples were brought plainly to our minds, and is it any wonder that our faith in the Bible grew stronger? I think not.

Banias, or Cesarea Philippi, is thought to be the scene of Christ's transfiguration, the place where his outward form was changed; for we read of his face shining as the sun and of his raiment being white as the light. Christ's presence was felt in Cesarea Philippi, for we read again that when he came into the coasts he asked his disciples these questions: "Whom do men say that I, the Son of man, am?" When they answered him, "he saith unto them, But whom say ye that I am? And Simon Peter answered and said, Thou art the Christ, the Son of the living God." No human being had made such a revelation to Simon Peter, but the "Father which is in heaven."

On the top of a hill near our camping place were seen the ruins of an old castle. Some of the party, accompanied by a guide, went up the hill to see them, and those of us who were left behind went to our tents and spent that time resting.

The men did not reach camp till late in the evening, and some of us feared an accident had happened, or the pathway to camp had been lost; but mealtime brought every one around the board, happy and in good spirits.

Bedtime came later that night than usual because of the delay, so we were the losers, for next morning we were not allowed to sleep any later than usual.

At this point our journey in Palestine ends, and now we enter Syria.

From Cesarea Philippi we rode up the side of Mount Hermon, said to be the highest mountain in Syria. On the top of it snow and ice are found the year round. In Bible times this mountain was sometimes called Sion, also Serion. It has several peaks, and upon one of them are to be found the ruins of a temple supposed to have been erected there years and years ago for the worship of Baal. Now Baal was an idol; so temples and altars erected for the worship of that god were usually built upon high places. We read that Josiah beat down the altars which had been erected "on top of the upper chambers of Ahaz." The Israelites were instructed to "utterly destroy all the places wherein the nations which ye shall possess served their gods, upon the high mountains, and upon the hills." The worship of Baal in those times was so great that human beings—sons of families—were offered as burnt offerings to him. No wonder instructions were given to "utterly destroy all the places."

We did not ride to the top of Mount Hermon, because it was not necessary; but a ridge to the right of it was crossed, and we found the way steep and wonderfully rough. Never before had we gone over such roads, and there was considerable danger connected with the trip. The Lord took care of us, as usual, and we came out all right.

Lunch was eaten that day near a Druse village. They are a people who greatly detest Christians, so we were very careful not to give occasion for offense. Our stop there was not any more agreeable to us than it seemed to be to them, so we were quite willing to ride on as soon as possible after luncheon.

In the afternoon we crossed the swiftly flowing river Pharpar. A number of Arab men, who were almost naked, led our horses through the rushing, dashing water, and it took but a little while for us to find that each man knew his business well. The water was quite deep, almost up to our feet, and the current was so swift it seemed the horses would surely go down stream instead of right across. We realized how necessary it was to have our horses led by men who not only knew the fording place, but who were strong and able to manage horses when in water. Those

Arabs assisted both men and women to cross over, and indeed not any one of the party could have crossed without help.

That night our camping place was close to the river and very near to a mountain village. We were now well on our way to Damascus. We found the road long and the ride extremely wearisome, with nothing special to attract our attention.

When the caravan road leading from Damascus to Egypt was gained, we were reminded of Saul and what befell him on his way to the same city. You remember how cruelly he had been acting, how he had put Christian men and women in prison, and then how he stood by and saw Stephen stoned? Well, the Lord knew how to stop Saul in his cruel work, for before the city was gained, and somewhere on the road I've been telling you about, we read that "suddenly there shined round about him a light from heaven: and he fell to the earth, and heard a voice saying unto him, Saul, Saul, why persecutest thou me?" And then for three days this man was blind, and those who were with him led him to the city. Instead of persecuting the Christians, as heretofore, Saul preached Christ; after which his life was in peril, for the Jews decided to kill him.

The exact spot where this great man was stricken down is not known, but we do know he journeyed on the road which led to Damascus.

· A large caravan of camels, on the way to Egypt, stopped to rest and feed close to where we were lunching. Such sights were quite common to us, and but little attention was paid to them. They journeyed on toward Egypt, and we moved on toward Damascus. When within a few miles of the city we halted, and camped there for the night.

The next morning every one in the party was anxious to leave camp early, but the dragoman seemed unusually anxious to take his time; so we were compelled to exercise patience. In very good time, however, we started on the way, and after getting a short distance from camp a view of the old city burst suddenly upon us. There were the domes and minarets pointing heavenward; and as we drew nearer and nearer to the city the groves, gardens and winding streams were seen. Truly the sight was a very beautiful one, and no doubt the ride across the desert plains helped us to enjoy the scene to its fullest extent. The dragoman was anxious to make as good an appearance going into the city as possible, so he rode on before and we all followed after. Finally the hotel was reached, and with joy each one dismounted, giving the horses over to the care of the men who were there waiting. That night we slept under a roof instead of under canvas, and it was the first time since leaving Jerusalem. I am not sure we slept any more soundly there than in our tents, but there was such a satisfaction in knowing that the roof which covered us was more than canvas, and that thieves could enter only at the door. For a night or two our shoes were left upon the floor instead of being placed under the pillow, and how pleasant it was to know the baggage was safe without being tied to the bedstead!

Perhaps you wonder what became of the afflicted one of the party. Well, she was taken right along with us to Damascus, and when it came time for us to leave the city both she and her friend remained behind, while we journeyed on and on.

There was great pleasure in being in comfortable, home-like quarters, and the drawing room was quite a lively place for a while. Our clothes looked the worse for wear, and they were exchanged for those which were not soiled and travel-stained. It was surprising to see what a change had been brought about in the appearance of each one, not only in dress but in looks, for everybody seemed bright and cheerful.

Miss W. was compelled to eat all of her meals in her own room, since she was unable to go from place to place. We did not forget the invalid, or neglect her either, and at such times as were convenient we gathered in her room. At the expiration of three days we journeyed on through Syria toward the seaport town of Beyrut, each night camping by the way.

Damascus is said to be the oldest city of the world. Way back in Abraham's time mention was made of it as being the home of Eliezer, his steward. A number of times Damascus is spoken of in the Bible, and we believe it was as flourishing a city then as it is these years.

The rivers Pharpar and Abana supply Damascus with water, and great canals convey it far and wide over the surrounding country. No doubt you have read about these two rivers in connection with the Bible story of Naaman the leper. He knew the rivers were beautifully clear, and his preference was to wash in them rather than in the water the prophet directed him to wash in for the cleansing of the leprosy.

There is a street in Damascus which is called Via Recta. It runs from the east to the west gate. We were told it was "the street called Straight." In Bible times the Lord directed Ananias in a vision to go into that street and make inquiry for Saul of Tarsus. Ananias was timid about going; Saul's reputation was not good, for it was known far and wide how he had been treating all who called upon the name of the Lord. But the timid feelings were cast aside and the desire of the Lord followed out. Saul was found and the message was delivered, and after Saul's sight had been restored he "arose and was baptized." After his conversion Saul "preached Christ in the synagogues." The Jews opposed him and watched day and night to take his life; "but Saul increased the more in strength, and confounded the Jews which dwelt at Damascus, proving that this is very Christ." When the danger of being killed was greatest, "then the disciples took him by night, and let him down by the wall in a basket," and by that means Saul's life was spared a while longer to preach boldly for Jesus.

A window was shown us, said to be the window from which Saul was let down on that memorable night. The houses of Ananias and Naaman were also shown, but we shall never know whether they were really the houses in which those Bible characters lived. Naaman's house had been turned into a hospital, and we hope many sufferers have been made well inside of its walls.

There were no beautiful residences to admire while passing along, and you can scarcely imagine how strange it seemed to look at high blank walls.

In the far East houses are built with a court—an enclosed space—and on all sides of it are doors which lead into different rooms. Our hotel had an upper story, and the stairway which led to it opened on one corner of the court.

Every one going into a house must first pass through a gate in the high wall. There are a great many references in the Bible to the courts of houses, and you know king Ahasuerus made a feast in a court. It was customary for the door of a court to be locked, and consequently a servant attended to the opening of it. You remember when Peter was placed in prison by Herod and guarded by four soldiers he was released from his chains and set at liberty by the angel of the Lord? Well, Peter came "to the house of Mary the mother of John, whose surname was Mark," and "knocked at the door of the gate, and a damsel came to hearken." These instances show that the custom of having houses with courts to-day is the custom of centuries ago.

The bazaars of Damascus are very highly spoken of all over the world, and every traveler is anxious to visit them soon after reaching the city. We found the bazaars to be shops like open stalls, in avenues roofed over. When a customer purchases goods he walks up to the stall and is waited upon by the merchant, who is usually sitting down cross-legged. The purchaser stands on the street, which is very narrow, and the throng of buyers and wayfarers have a good chance to jostle him about unpleasantly. Merchants make much ado in selling their goods, for they talk furiously. To me it seemed a fight was brewing; but by and by the sale was completed and quiet reigned until another purchaser happened along. We wanted to purchase a few silk handkerchiefs, and before an attempt at a sale was made we were furnished with a cup of coffee each; after which an effort was made to sell the articles. Sales are not always made, for the buyer is not always pleased with the goods.

You may wonder how large the cups were, so I'll just tell you they held perhaps two tablespoonfuls of coffee ready to drink. That may seem like a very little bit, but it was quite enough, for we had to get rid of grounds too. In that country coffee is pounded in a mortar, making the grain as fine as powder. After having been boiled the mixture is sweetened, and then you get rid of it as best you can. A very strange custom you will think, but in time one becomes used to it.

While walking along we noticed some of the bazaars were without salesmen, and upon inquiry found the men had gone to the mosque for prayers. No matter when the hour of prayer came, business was cast aside, and away they went. Could not many Christians learn a lesson from the Mohammedans to-day? Surely they could.

The rattle of wagons is not heard in those roofed streets, but donkeys and camels quietly make their way

Water Seller.

through the crowd, not caring whether a person is stepped upon or not.

A missionary to the Jews, from London, England, made the acquaintance of our party, and through his kindness we were permitted to visit some of the best private houses in the city. Space will not allow me to tell you what was seen there, but before leaving the city of Damascus I want to tell you about the man who is in the picture. He is a water seller who goes along the streets selling water to those who desire a drink. Do you see the cup in his outstretched hand? And there upon his back is the leather bottle which holds the water. When walking along he calls out in loud tones, "Let him that is athirst come and drink;" and then comes a great noise from the knocking together of the tin cups. I do not know whether the man sells much water or not, for we did not stand still long enough for us to watch him.

Many years ago a great many Christians lived in Damascus, but the Moslems burned a portion of the city in which they lived, and thousands were put to death. The Christian population is now on the increase, and there is safety on the streets of Damascus for all Christian people. Missionaries have worked faithfully, scattering the good seed there. May the old and young alike pray the Lord to bless all efforts for good; and, little children, may the Lord help you all to get the missionary spirit, so that some day you may go forth and battle for the right.

CHAPTER XII.

Farewell to Damascus.—Ain Fijeh.—Quarrelsome Arabs.—Onward to Baalbek.—A Friendly Arab Family.—On the Mountains of Lebanon.—Baalbek.—Rejected Stone.— From Baalbek to Beyrut. — My Horse John.—Homeward Bound.

ADIEU was said to Damascus with its mosques, bazaars, orchards and winding streams. We left it never expecting to look again upon the city which the natives call "paradise on earth."

The day was delightful, and the scenery along the greater part of the way was quite different from that which we had been accustomed to seeing. The grass was beautifully green, and fruit trees were in splendid condition. The swift-flowing river was, in a measure, instrumental in clothing the trees with foliage and giving the grass its beautiful verdure; but behind all the hand of the Lord was seen.

Noontime came, and we rested not far from a small village called Ain Fijeh, very close to a fountain with the same name. Many years ago a temple stood at that place and people went there to worship. Now it is in ruins, but even yet many Mohammedans go there. While we stood by looking at them, they bowed down on their faces, saying aloud their studied prayers. A great body of water gushed out of a cave near by. It went dashing and splashing along a few yards, then joined a small branch, when the two made one river.

Did you ever watch a great volume of water as it dashed over everything which happened in its way? If you did, then you can imagine how much interested we grown up men and women were at the sight before us. That was a charming spot for travelers to tarry for the noonday rest, and yet the very name of Ain Fijeh brings thoughts exceedingly unpleasant.

Our luncheon was eaten in a field of beautiful green,—a cornfield. The dragoman hired a corner of it from the owner expressly for our use. It seemed hardly right to use a grain field in that way, but there was no other place for so large a party, and since arrangements had been made we settled down to enjoy the rest which was needed. The villagers seemed very much interested in us, more so than common, and during the entire meal watched us very closely. There was a wonderful chattering among them, and there seemed decided indications of displeasure; but since we were unable to understand their language we were entirely ignorant as to what irritated them.

The meal was eaten with a relish, notwithstanding the scowling faces which were looking on. The usual length of time was taken for rest; the dragoman awakened from his nap and gave the order to start. Soon after each person went where the horses were waiting, which place was at the foot of a very steep hill, where the ladies found rocks large enough to mount the horses from. Since the dragoman was not needed he remained back—as we supposed—

to pay for the use of the field. After having arranged ourselves ready for the onward march, we waited for our guide to come and lead us on through the unknown country. Instead of going with us, as had been his custom, he called in loud tones, "Ride on and follow the road." There were sixteen of us now, and one just as ignorant as the other of the language and country. We did not fancy starting out alone, but the order was given and we obeyed, riding fast or slow just as it suited us.

A change in the road seemed confusing, and we all decided to go no farther without a guide. The summit of the hill was reached by that time, and you can scarcely imagine our surprise, on looking back, to see the dragoman completely surrounded by the villagers. He was unable to turn from right to left. Truly, like sheep without a shepherd were we.

Now, what was to be done,—stand still and wait? Yes, it was all we were able to do, for we knew not where to go. By this time we noticed the villagers were wild with excitement. Men and women ran up the hill with clubs and pickaxes raised in the air; children came running too, each armed with stones. Every one of them seemed determined to hurt us, if possible. Their voices were pitched high, and such a furious set of people I had never seen before. We were a scared set of tourists. To add to our dismay, stones were hurled in our midst. Many of them hit the poor horses, my own faithful animal being among the number. I shall never forget how suddenly he turned and what a narrow escape I had from going headlong over the side of the hill. I begged to be taken from my horse, but was not allowed to be upon my feet for fear of being in greater danger.

That was a very distressing time for us, boys and girls, for we did not expect to escape without injury. The dear Lord was good, for his watchful eye was over us and every one quit the place unharmed. My nervous system received a severe shock, which it has taken all of these years to recover from. The Arabs did not release the dragoman until he paid them a large sum of money, and at the end of our journey each one of the party was requested to pay a certain sum of money extra to help pay for the release of our guide.

Ain Fijeh had lost all attractions for us, and as soon as possible we rode away, leaving its disagreeable inhabitants behind, hoping never to be in such an unpleasant situation again. It was the first day of April. Had we been in America, we would have thought the people were having a little fun at our expense; but not so there, for money was what they desired, and money they received before we were allowed to go free.

As we proceeded on our way to camp great ledges of rocks were passed over. Sometimes we rode through green fields, when our mind was carried back to the lunching place and the yelling villagers. My memory of the country through which we passed is not vivid, for my mind and feelings then were not in trim to enjoy either the country or a ride through it. The camping place for that night is spoken of as being fine, but I cannot testify as to its beauty. One thing I am sure of,—that our rest during that night was much disturbed by thoughts of the day's experience.

We left camp early next morning, and to our sorrow the rain came down in torrents. Oh, how unpleasant it was! We had no desire to visit the tomb of Abel, which we passed. We rode on, preferring to visit a place of shelter and stay there while the rain continued to fall. It was useless, however, to think of that pleasure; so we made the best of the situation, feeling sure that only a few more days of hard riding and exposure were in store for us, when our journey through the strange land would be ended.

Bad weather never seemed to bring changes in our programme of travel, so we bravely weathered the rain which had continued to fall, and onward we rode toward Baalbek. The air had become uncomfortably chilly, and a great desire for a sheltered place was created within us. It seemed to be the order of our trip to have unpleasant things happening, and for that particular day an accident was recorded; not a serious one, yet an accident.

We were riding by a swiftly flowing mountain river, when the horse which an English lady was riding made a misstep and both of them went down into the water. The animal was unable to help himself and it was therefore necessary for some of the men to render assistance. In good time both horse and rider reached land without injury.

Wet clothing was the result of that accident, and now for certain a good, warm fire was needed. Many of us could sympathize with the lady, for we were in the same condition, although our clothing became wet from the rain and hers from the river; therefore we knew, to our sorrow, how uncomfortable she was. Not any of the company had much to say while riding along, but we kept up a wonderful thinking.

Our first stopping place after the accident was in a small village where the people were unusually friendly. We were invited into their homes and we gladly accepted the kind invitation. Dripping wet we rode through the little entrance-gate into the court, and while the rain was pouring down upon us we dismounted, only too thankful to be under roof, where, for a short season at least, the rain would cease to beat upon us. Our joy was great when a fire was started in the fireplace in one corner of a room. I can see that room yet—in my mind's eye—cheerless and unattractive, not a window was to be seen, and in the wall were hollow places where the family slept at night. But the shelter and the fire we wanted, and that we had, caring but little for the dirt and the cheerless home.

The ladies seemed to think the room was all their own, for immediately they took possession of it, each one getting as close to the fire as possible, all intent on drying their soaking wet garments. The native women were very much interested in our clothing, examining each piece with a great deal of pleasure. They had a strong desire to converse with us, but there was entirely too much difference in our language, for not one of us could speak Arabic. They jabbered away at us, and we stood smiling like a lot of schoolgirls.

One old woman couldn't stand it to be near and not converse, so she went after the dragoman, brought him in and used him as an interpreter. The conversation was laughable, but not of long duration, for it was time to leave there and ride on.

The men sat in a room adjoining ours, and I believe it was much dirtier; but we were quite well used to filth by that time, so it failed to be a rarity.

Other travelers were resting in the same house, and in the court could be seen horses, donkeys and camels. It was quite amusing to watch a clumsy camel get through the small entrance gate to the court. It was first compelled to get down upon its knees to have the burden removed, after which some manœuvering was necessary to get the animal inside, for the large hump was very much in the way. The stupid animal entered by and by, and we saw it no more, for by that time we rode away from the house of the kind Arab people.

We had traveled twenty-five miles during the day, wet to the skin and chilled to the bone. Late in the evening we reached camp, with a longing desire for a good, warm fire. Money could not purchase such a luxury there, so we were compelled to be reconciled to the surroundings.

We seemed to be unfortunate that night, for during the day some of the pack-mules had fallen into the water; so the tents and bedding were wet through and through. Our tent and some bedclothes were among the wet ones, and I'll tell you, children, our comfort for that night did not seem very flattering. It was very hard work to have cheerful faces, and it was a great deal harder to keep from wishing we were at home, where there was no end of comfort. We crept into our little beds, shivering, hoping to be warm at least by morning.

All night long the rain came down fast, and about midnight the side of our tent blew in, making the situation more unpleasant. We called the dragoman, telling him of our perplexing condition, and he in turn called up the poor, shivering Arab servants, who pounded the tent pins down more tightly; after which quiet reigned and an effort was made to sleep. We were on the Mountains of Lebanon and the air was cold, so we expected to shiver as did the Arab men.

The next morning early we started for Baalbek, notwithstanding the rain storm which was still in progress. We mounted our horses in a tent that morning. The horses seemed wonderfully large standing there waiting for the riders. The saddles were dripping wet, and of course the poor animals were in like condition. That morning the dragoman's counts and my leap did not come out even, for when he said, "Now ready," I had not reached the back of my faithful friend. But with patience on the part of the guide, and quite an effort on my part, the sitting place was gained and we rode on out in the rain.

As we journeyed along snow commenced falling, and we wondered what next. Such a discouraged set of tourists you never saw, I know. We were ill prepared for winter weather, and the Australian lady who had never seen snow was getting all she desired of it. Her wraps were quite thin, and, like myself, she shivered as we went along.

My hands were not as well protected as they might have been had we thought of snow. As it was I wore a thin pair of knit mittens which were wet during the entire ride of sixteen miles.

By this time you have learned that people who go long journeys become tired and are liable to have accidents happen them too. It is plain to be seen that one must be prepared for anything, and if possible be cheerful under all circumstances.

The sun did not shine all of the time, and we knew to our sorrow what it meant to travel when rain was pouring down upon us. On the way to Baalbek our ride was as unpleasant as could well be imagined. Snow and rain were our portion many miles. The little flakes fell thick and fast. Occasionally they found their way to our neck, where they melted, leaving the water to trickle down our back, making us still more chilly and uncomfortable. It would weary you if I were to make any further attempt to tell you of that very unpleasant ride. There was genuine pleasure however in looking forward to the time when the village should be gained and we be under the shelter of a roof; and as we rode on and on it was a satisfaction to know every mile took us nearer and nearer the resting place. At last the columns of the "Great Temple" were seen in the distance. Immediately we took fresh courage and urged our horses to greater speed. By and by the village was gained, and to our delight the dragoman drew rein and we all dismounted in front of a rough looking building, bearing the name of "Hotel," which was to be our home while in the village of ruined temples. Everything around it seemed gloomy and cheerless; but we wasted no time in looking at the surroundings, for we were anxious to go where wet clothing could be removed.

Husband found, to his sorrow, that boots were very good to hold water, for on placing his feet upon the ground the water overflowed and rushed out of the top of them; so you may see what a distressed condition he was in.

When a room was assigned us we were surprised to see it so large and with such a little bit of furniture in it. The floor was stone and carpetless; two windows were in the room, but they were curtainless, and there was no stove in which to make fire. We needed dry clothing badly, but the baggage had not been brought up, for it was far back on the mountain. Now what was to be done? ·Well, each person settled that question for himself. Some concluded to go to bed and stay there until the baggage was brought them. We called for a fire; a foolish thing to do when there was no stove, you may think; but it came to us all right in two iron pans with coals red hot. Immediately after, each piece of clothing was removed, the water wrung out, and then it was held piece by piece over the coals to dry. The task was not an easy one, I assure you, and both of us were kept busy for a while. We were quite comfortable long before our baggage came, for the men were four hours behind time.

The sun was not hid under a cloud all of that day, for during the afternoon it shone beautifully, which brought joy to our hearts. We did not remain indoors long, for all were anxious to see the great ruins of Baalbek, which at one time were temples erected for the worship of Baal. They have been the wonder of all ages, and nowhere in the world can more extensive ruins be seen. People travel thousands of miles to see them. The largest cut stones in the world are to be seen in these temples, and it is a great mystery to know how they were placed there. A quarry from which they were taken is not very far from the village, and one large stone is still there, having never been removed by the workmen. The stone chips lie about and one can scarcely realize the fact that many, many years have gone by since the chisel and hammer have been used upon it.

I shall not begin to describe the ruined temples, for it might not interest the greater number of the little readers, and to tell you about the finely chiseled marble columns would occupy too much space. The population of Baalbek was not very large, and there was nothing attractive about the dwelling houses, for they were free from ornamentation, low, and covered with flat straw roofs. After a hard rain men go on the housetop with large wooden rollers to press out the water. If it were allowed to remain in the straw long it would drip down into the living rooms and be unpleasant for the family.

As a result of the exposure of our trip from Damascus to Baalbek, I was taken sick with a hard chill and high fever; but with the free use of medicines the fever was broken and I was enabled to travel on with the rest of the party. After the ruins of the village were seen there were no further attractions for tourists. So one bright beautiful morning we left with everybody in a cheerful mood and very anxious to go on to the next place, which would end our horseback riding.

We went direct from Baalbek to Beyrut, camping by the way and taking two days for the journey. All of the party were in good humor and quite cheerful, as I said before, and even the horses traveled better; so the good feeling seemed general.

We camped on the mountains and had pure fresh air to breathe. Luncheon was eaten in a stone khan, and when I look back to that time I can see sixteen weary travelers sitting on benches against the wall, listening to the dragoman talk, telling us how much money was due him. We knew he had no right to demand it, yet for the sake of peace the money was handed over to him. After a short rest we all moved onward toward a large town by the name of Zableh. The road was rocky and steep, and the horses' feet clattered as they walked up the street, which seemed more like a stairway.

The people seemed friendly, which at first surprised us; but we found later on that a goodly number of the inhabitants were Christians. Missionaries were settled in that town, and it was plain to be seen that where the Bible is taught a kindlier feeling toward mankind is manifested. Several years ago the town suffered badly from the Druses, a set of people who live in the Mountains of Lebanon; they set fire to it and burned it down. Since then the town has been rebuilt and seems in a prosperous condition.

Our last day's ride was delightful, and the roads were now good enough for any one. We passed from the stormy weather of winter into summer and beautiful sunshine, and how pleasant it seemed! The green grass, the fruit trees, many of which had fruit upon them, all helped us to forget the snowstorm of Lebanon and the cheerless country which had been traveled over only a few days before.

As we neared the city of Beyrut every turn in the road gave us a better glimpse of the place for which we were aiming. The pleasant little country residences by the way received but little notice. We were bound for the place where letters from dear ones at home were awaiting us. The city was not so far away now, and before we were aware of it our horses went galloping down the streets,— there at last! Yes, sure enough, for the horses had stopped and we found ourselves in front of the hotel, and the twenty-one days of riding ended.

I was greatly attached to my horse, which you will remember I had named John, and a feeling of sadness filled my heart when the servant led him away. I looked after the animal and thought how faithfully he had carried me upon his back, and in the twenty-one days' ride had not shown a sign of being tricky. Cautiously he had picked his way over the most dangerous places, and when rivers were to be forded he walked into the water and bore me safe to the opposite side. Every step he took seemed to tell me he knew I was timid and that he must therefore be very careful. I looked after him, and with a silent goodbye stepped into the hotel and to my room.

Beyrut is beautifully situated by the Mediterranean Sea, with its streets sloping down, down to the beach, where we loved to stand and watch the water roll and dash.

In the city are missions where the people are taught the way to God, and young girls are taught to sing the songs of Zion.

The lady who had broken her limb was pleasantly situated at the hotel, and I am sure you never saw a person more pleased to meet friends than was Miss W. to see us. She had been fortunate in procuring the services of a good physician who lived in Beyrut. He had placed her limb in a plaster Paris case and she was getting along as well as might be expected.

Our hotel was right on the beach, and when sitting on the upper porch one could see beyond the waters of the bay far out on the "great sea." It was quite pleasant to sit there and watch the ships in the distance as they glided over the water. I remarked, "How very smooth and quiet the sea is to-day. Surely a pleasant time to board the ship is in store for us." A missionary lady replied, "Possibly by two o'clock the sea will be very wild." And I thought it could hardly be possible, for sailing time was near at hand.

Having nothing else to do I decided to watch the sea. Away off in the distance a breaker rolled up; by and by a few more were seen; and then I thought the lady knew what she was talking about, for one by one the white-capped waves broke upon the shore before me, and the ship, which was anchored perhaps a mile out, was made to move about uneasily. When the hour of departure drew near seventeen people besides the boatmen took seats in two rowboats. The men rowed toward the ship with a will, while the water dashed about the little boats ladened with precious freight. The ship was gained in safety; shortly after the whistle blew, and we were on our way home. Many times we had longed for the day when our faces would be turned in the direction of home, and now a silent prayer for safety was breathed.

The sea voyage was rather a pleasant one, and in due time we reached Smyrna, where many of our traveling companions took ship for Constantinople and the rest of us went on to Trieste.

The first day of May we took passage on the steamship Werra, and for six days she rolled and pitched because of a terrible storm on the Atlantic. Of course I was seasick, and for three days ate not a mouthful of food. When the storm subsided my desire for food returned, and from that on I was able to go on deck. Eleven days were spent at sea, and not one day was it quiet. When we landed at New York our hearts were full of gratitude to the Lord for his tender, watchful care over us; for we were conscious of his presence all the way and knew he would bring us home safely.

Now, dear children, the task which was undertaken so reluctantly is ended. Yet I cannot refrain from saying the work grew to be a pleasure to me; and now it is given to you with the thought and hope that some little word may have been written which will lead you to seek a better life. Some one has said, "It is the greatest pleasure of living, to win souls to Christ." And should I be the instrument by which one boy or girl is brought to Christ, my labor has not been in vain. And now may the kind Heavenly Father bless you and keep your tender feet from treading the paths of sin and wickedness.

THE END.

www.ingramcontent.com/pod-product-compliance
Lightning Source LLC
Chambersburg PA
CBHW021351230426
43666CB00006B/481